HOMESPUN HARMONY

HOMESPUN HARMONY

A BOOK OF POETRY
DORIS KOEHLER

Charleston, SC
www.PalmettoPublishing.com

Homespun Harmony
Copyright © 2023 by Doris Koehler

All rights reserved
No portion of this book may be reproduced, stored in a retrieval system, or transmitted in any form by any means–electronic, mechanical, photocopy, recording, or other–except for brief quotations in printed reviews, without prior permission of the author.

First Edition

Paperback: 979-8-8229-1292-2

HOMESPUN HARMONY

A BOOK OF POETRY
DORIS KOEHLER

Charleston, SC
www.PalmettoPublishing.com

Homespun Harmony
Copyright © 2023 by Doris Koehler

All rights reserved
No portion of this book may be reproduced, stored in a retrieval system, or transmitted in any form by any means–electronic, mechanical, photocopy, recording, or other–except for brief quotations in printed reviews, without prior permission of the author.

First Edition

Paperback: 979-8-8229-1292-2

A Day in the Life

A day in the life of a fireman
On call and ready to serve
Danger and rescue awaits
For all of us safety preserve

A day in the life of an educator
Preparation for years did earn
The privilege to instruct our youth
As well as adults with desires to learn

A day in the life of a senior
Tasks now consume the whole day
When once you did them in minutes
That pace now not suits your way

A day in the life of young parents
So busy with family all day
This a most important investment
When close attention they constantly pay

A day in the life of a homeless
Shelter and food for just now
A struggle to acquire the basics
Much more they seldom allow

A day in the life of a doctor
Curing the ills of all the land
A life dedicated to serving
Days and nights with a helping hand

A day in the life of a policeman
Keeping law and order for all
Engaging in dangers of the lawless
Each time they take one more call

A day in the lives of a clergy
With flocks to tend and lead
While waning attendance continues
With the world's healing such a need

A day in the life of a farmer
A day in the life of our savior
With faith sows seed each season
Whose day is filled with us all

Trusting the weather to nourish
Continues to fill all our needs
A love of the land is the reason
Always there to catch as we fall

A Helping Hand to the Hurting

When thinking or doing
A concept to heed
A slant to observe
A thoughtful opening lead

Addressing situations
With only one's thought
Not being attentive to
Others as we ought

When approaching a person
With a purpose to ease
A ministry to comfort
That person to please

Awareness of struggles
Or signs of distress
One may be harboring
Before speaking access

With love and care
Ask a blessing to serve
The needs of this person
And their situation observed

Self cannot enter
This calling to aid
It's all about others
When a cry for help made

We all have this challenge
Likely to meet any day
With a major concern
Or some minor display

So rise to the occasion
Ask God to grant a word
To give comfort and peace
To the cry we have heard

A New Day

Yesterday is past and gone
Today a new sunrise came
Forget what's taken place before
And do not harbor blame

If we retain the former things
That happen every day
Soon we will be loaded down
And cannot see the way

Take the good and leave the bad
This we learn from each
As another day then draws
Another opportunity to teach

The whole of all the days we've spent
Creates a way of living
So pick and choose the wisest
And the wisdom that they're giving

Soon a pattern clearly forms
You will simply choose this way
Without consciously recognizing
Your will create a good day

A Part of Each, the Whole of All

One part of a family
Each one has a place
Combining the lives
Signified by a face

Each has a part
In this daily life
Supporting and sharing
The good and the strife

As is with a fellowship
Where we worship and share
As Jesus has taught us
Joys and burdens to bear

A community as well
Joins all to combine
A diverse group to develop
And talents to find

In government we strive
To choose people to lead
Making decisions of wisdom
For good of all not greed

These all part of the world
With many cultures combined
Love one another our goal
Only through grace we will find

The whole of universe
God created it all
Surrounds all of being
All a part though small

Each single person
Should honor his plan
This would be ideal
For the world and man

A Poem for Tra-Tra

When you were born
We were so glad
We looked at you
You weren't too bad

When your ma upon you glazed
She turned to pa and he was dazed
Knowing nothing else to do
They took you home to watch you too

As years went by, you grew and grew
Every year there were more you knew
Till now you nice, slim, and tall
But too you've got a lot of gall

You'll turn fo'teen
In a coupla days
God help you then
To mend your ways

Just be real good
And don't be coarse
Be a precious thing
Just like your good aunt Doris

A Tribute to Mother

There is mother wisdom
There is mother care
There is mother love
Found everywhere

The love of a mother
A bond forever
In all walks of life
A bond hard to sever

To guide and to nurture
From conception begins
A commitment for life
Into the world she then sends

From infancy to childhood
A mother remains
Connected and attentive
A heart that retains

Through joys and some sorrows
Her love sees it through
Prayerfully seeking answers
What a mother should do

A thing to remember
Jesus' mother's pain
As she witnessed his suffering
Preventing his death in vain

Motherhood a blessing
A gift from above
To cherish and nurture
And accept with love

Advent

The turkey eaten
The guests have gone
Football nonstop
On this weekend long

Shopping started
Decorating begun
Travel planning
Colored lights strung

Oh, but wait!
This brings us to
The advent season
That's what we're to do

Preparations to make
For the great event
The birth of Christ
God his son sent

Keeping in mind
This blessed gift
God's love and grace
Voice should lift

The true beauty
Of this time of year
Can only come
If of his birth we hear

A savior born
Our choirs sing
Worship the child
That hope will bring

This busy world
Sometimes fail pay
Faithful homage
To this blessed day

This my prayer
For all the earth
To know the joy
Of this holy birth

APPRECIATION

Degrees of appreciation
A very general term
As people are diverse
Relative to concern

A rich man's appreciation
May require material gain
While a working breadwinner
May be struggling in vain

The solution may sound simple
To be satisfied is tough
But this doesn't apply
When "what is" is not enough

Working people's gains
Provide most basic needs
Within this class needs vary
Too much begets some greeds

Few people satisfied with little
For material gain obsessed
Becomes an accepted term
A difficulty to address

This and age-old situation
There will always be the poor
As well as many rich
All that want or need more

Prayers for needy a good think
Lifting them up is also needed
If God gives the wisdom
Just basic needs could be exceeded

Our prayers for this wisdom
Should pass our lips each day
Until every child of God
Would receive this golden ray

As We Journey Here

Whose gray hair is in my comb
Whose picture in the mirror
Whose meds for aches and pains and such
From the self do peer

Whose are all these friends
Waling stooped and slow
People my same age
They say I speak too low

These hands with age spots
They can't belong to me
Double chin and thinning hair
And sight that does not see

The day I dreamed of sleeping in
Has come for it's our time
Now I awake at 4:00 a.m.
Bright-eyed and feeling fine

Keeping notes to remember
Every single task at hand
Writing every need down
No clue why here I stand

Make no mistake I love life
It just takes a little longer
To process thoughts and deeds
We're not getting any stronger

The reactions of the young
Alike my youthful time
Could not for the life of me
Understand this pace of mine

The wisdom that I've acquired
Seems useless to the young
But then required at a time
To the family I'm among

The joy outweighs the aging
The precious family time
To be a part of the sharing
An answered prayer of mine

We laugh at all the things we do
We swore would never be
But so grateful to be able
To live all this to see

God has been so good to us
Sometimes we did not know
He always had a hand on us
When our own way we did go

So all the gray hairs, wrinkles
Are part of who we are
Loving every age we've been
Together come this far

We plan to be around some time
As long as God intends
To enjoy and savor life
The time on him depends

When we leave to join him
According to his time
He will perfect us to will
Wrinkles he would not mind

ATTENTION

Attention is a busy word
It's used in many ways
All things need attention
You'll find this throughout your day

The first thing in the morning
Your body must have aid
Every day of your life
Attention must be paid

Your property included
Also family needs to meet
So much we take for granted
Until we come upon defeat

Your mind and spirit also
Need tending all the while
To round out your living
And create a moral style

While through this world we're passing
We've chances to attention pay
Some we recognize and address
Others fall by the way

When children join our daily lives
The attention mounts to a degree
That sometimes overwhelms us
As all new ventures can be

This must be approached with faith
A young life to shape and mold
This is a lifetime process
Outcome in our hands we hold

The same care and love apply
When we're in our autumn days
The same attention then comes back
To give care in many, many ways

How ideal this world of God could be
If we could follow all his ways
Pay attention to attention
And pray for serving him all days

AUTUMN

A special time of year
The days so crisp and cool
The turning leaves create
The landscape a topaz jewel

A remembrance to veterans
An annual tribute to those
Who bravely served our country
When any need arose

Fall harvests reap rich produce
With bounty we share so free
To savor at the table
By family and friends that be

This time of year we gather
Thankful on Thanksgiving Day
For all our earthly blessings
Our prayers of thanks we pray

Hunting and football season
Keep some entertained quite well
While festivals favored by others
With seasonal flavors to tell

Bonfires and fireplaces fired
As we gather around the glow
Bringing comfort and warming
And a peace so good to know

AWARENESS

Look around
What do you see
The world out there
For you and for me

To let it pass by
Not see what there is
All it has for us
What a plan was his

Nature and people
All in his scheme
So overwhelming
When clearly seen

So many species
From great to small
All have a purpose
And God loves it all

We are among this
A part of the whole
Living within it
A harmonious goal

Peace is the ideal
For which we strive
Considering each being
With love will thrive

Each petal, each breath
So precious to all
A hug or a smile
Anytime there's a call

Observe these chances
To fill these needs
Awareness for good
Then follow good deeds

BACK TO WRITING

Gathering words to make appoint
Usually a simple task
Then a writer's block appears
The mind a blank quite vast

So today the story goes
As I grasp for words evading
Warming to the keyboard
Before what's left begins fading

So very much has happened
Since I've had the pleasure of writing
My mind can't take all in at once
Now that the holidays are quieting

A beautiful holiday it is
As the new year is yet to come
The savior's birth remembered
Pray, it's a revelation to some

Family, food, and worship
Gifting, visits, in addition
So much joy surrounding
Much pleasure from tradition

The new year in just days
When we begin with goals
Daunting days we may be facing
As the new year days unfold

God was here for all others
He will be here for now
And when all is said and done
He will be with us is his vow

Pass this on to others
So they, too, may be content
Confident of his grace
This always his intent

Baptism Day

Ms. Tatum and Ms. McKinley
Receiving water and the word
Few other gifts will ever
Compare with this, your Lord

He is the water of each life
So you will never thirst
If you always keep his word
Consider these things first

Today becoming children of God
He holds you in his arms
Surrounding you with love and peace
In sunshine and through storms

All the steps you ever take
In the stages of your growth
These truths will always be
His sacred promised oath

This journey that you now begin
His gift upon your heart
Nourish it with hope and faith
Living in grace now starts

Surround your life with God and good
Always giving God the glory
Avoiding many regrets and grief
When you live your life's story

BAPTISM DAY

To sweet baby Lawrence

Today with water and the word
The sealed promise granted you
A child of God forevermore
In all you say and do

Call on him your whole life through
No matter when or where
He will guide you if you ask
Always remember he is there

BATTLES

Battles large and battles small
To each calls us to be bold
Chosen or placed upon us
The struggles still withhold

Nationwide or personal
Battles of life bring pain
Illness, war, or living life
The efforts still remain

Battles to some a way of life
Others avoid that path
Trust in God and his wisdom
Avoid conflict and wrath

Some lives are constant battles
To an aggressive-natured one
When failing to consider
Those affected when all done

There's no need for troubled battles
When we leave them up to him
Forgetting foolish power plays
No gain from a hollow win

Recognizing others' battles
Surrounding us each day
Reaching out to comfort
In our own responding way

There are battles fought for good
Evil forces to remove
These are our commission
Peace, not war to prove

Inner battles thought overwhelming
Until we seek the reason why
This troubled thing that grieves us
Dealt with where our demons lie

As long as man walks this earth
Battles will ensue
Some are valid, others not
Man must do what man must do

Being Busy

So busy being busy
No time for being still
What a way to function
Our agenda we must fill

The media promotes "busy"
A mindset we buy into
Only we ourselves obey
With busy things to do

Examine only the required
To maintain a stable pace
With all "extras" stripped
And our reality faced

Being busy, a diversion
Avoiding tasks at hand
Choosing not to fulfill
Thus we take a stand

Rethinking is the answer
Be true to what serves best
Not what another chooses
Mimicry put to rest

Opportunities in abundance
To partake of tempting things
Until one too many
A stressful end now brings

Scripture tells of peace
The answer we all know
He leaves us with his peace
Overcrowded lives must go

BLESSINGS

It's blessed to awake each day
And blessings continue thus
Each breath we take not thinking
A blessing granted us

Shelter, food, and family
Our needs are always met
Far beyond necessity
Bounties and beyond we get

Privileges taken for granted
Enjoyed without a thought
From the day that we are born
Not as grateful as we ought

A country free of persecution
We are free to come and go
Speak freely of our convictions
A freedom many do not know

We must treasure our freedom
It was paid for with much pain
A most precious, well-fought blessing
By far too many brave men to name

Not only blessed this Veterans Day
Recognizing just once a year
But every living moment
Give thanks for freedom, dear

With this blessing lives are good
We have much to give thanks for
Thanksgiving thus as we well should
Celebrate consciously our great store

There are little blessings constant
Some we see and some not
Heaped on us when we least see
The blessings that we've got

Blessings Bestowed

As we awake each morning
Our first thought should be
Gratitude for a night of rest
And another beautiful sunrise see

Safe in our homes protected
In a country free and strong
We must never take for granted
This blessing granted for so long

God seeks to be in all our lives
The center in each home
Without him always as the head
We're without a cornerstone

The blessings far outweigh our worth
He is always there to seek
If we trust his promises
Giving strength when we are weak

Practice loving and forgiving
As he loves and forgives us all
Patience, kindness, and sharing
The fruits of his loving call

Reach out to all around you
Ready to share his word
The greatest gift you will ever give
To each soul his word has heard

Books are the carriers of civilization. Without books, history is silent, literature dumb, science crippled, thought and speculation at a standstill.... They are the engines of change (as the poet said), windows on the world lighthouses erected in the sea of time.

—Barbara W. Tuchman,
popular American historian and author (1912–1989)

BRANCHES

Compare people to branches
That extend from the trunk of a tree
The strength of a given limb
Depends on roots and growth that be

Well-nurtured trees will flourish
Their potential to grow tall
Trimming, shaping, pruning
Spreading, furnishing shade for all

Think of people, think of branches
How different yet the same
All have a shape and a reason
Determined how they're trained

Some branches stretch to heights
Beyond the reach of all
Some drape and sway to breezes
Like people, short and tall

A home for squirrels and birds
Or whatever chooses such
Providing food and shelter
Branches provide so much

So when you see a tree
With branches all askew
Take time to find a reason
You may change your point of view

Many lessons taught by nature
Creation, quite a show
"His eye is on the sparrow"
And on us as well, you know!

Canton 2012

Heading southwest from Canton
Down forty-five in the rain
A load of treasures
Gone shopping again

From collectibles to metal
For Christmas and fall
Our visa cards smoking
We shared them with all

Met many nice people
Bought gifts for many
Good food and great friends
Spent down to the penny

Thank God for the rain
The road washed clean
The hayfields absorbing
Good grazing foreseen

The distance 320
A good time to chat
We did that nonstop
All four excel at that

For mother and daughter
So special to spend
Quality time to catch up
So soon it did end

The trip a success
Our spouses await
God grant a safe trip
Not returning too late

On the occasion of our mother-daughter shopping trip to Canton, Texas. September 26–29 2012. (Donna and Edie and Robin and Doris). I thank you all for a wonderful time!

Doris Koehler

CELEBRATE

Celebrate mornings
Each day you awake
This great gift of life
Never lightly do take

Celebrate family
How precious are they
Honor each member
In your own unique way

Celebrate your home
A haven for rest
Welcome your neighbor
Share of your best

Celebrate your labor
Be thankful for strength
The ability to toil
Providing at length

Celebrate rest
To regain your pace
A very wise practice
When more tasks to face

Celebrate friends
So precious to you
Treat them with kindness
Also constantly renew

The best celebration
Is surely to come
In our heavenly home
When life here is done

So celebrate living
With goodness and love
Each day you awake
Thank your Father above

Celebrate Joy Because...

Celebrate joy
In each shower of rain
In sunrises and sunsets
In waving fields of grain

Celebrate joy
In a good book to read
A visit from a friend
To witness a good deed

Celebrate joy
At the birth of a child
On the first day of school
A baby fawn in the wild

Celebrate joy
On a job well done
A good doctor's report
A vacation that's fun

Celebrate joy
When a family unites
A flag flying high
Of soft candlelight

Celebrate joy
When children play
When songs are sung
When you've had a good day

Celebrate joy
When a life is lived well
On a regular day
When there's good news to tell

Celebrate joy
That scripture assures
The source of true joy
From God's love outpours

Changing Seasons

Like nature's changing seasons
In life we change as well
Taking heed from nature
There is much there to tell

The season of our youth
So free and fresh like spring
Followed then by summer warmth
That midlife patterns bring

The autumn season then arrives
As with us changes take place
Reflections and reminiscing
When the "golden years" we face

When winter years we enter
With the wisdom of the times
When we were all of the above
Savoring all in our primes

When thinking back on seasons
And the best of each we glean
The whole of life we cherish
In this great plan we've seen

If in each season we accept
The inevitable come what may
Embracing every good thing
Make every day our best day

We should remember always
Who designed this great plan
Enduring, perfect for all time
For nature, beast, and man

Charles Roy Cook

Birthday boy child of God

We celebrate your first year
You have grown by leaps and bounds
Now to explore all you see
Next weightlifting with Dad's pounds

Big sister there to lead and guide
Discovering toddler one-on-one
Soon your mom must let you stray
They will all be glad to join your fun

Grandparents, aunts, uncles, and cousins
Will follow you through it all
Then one day to our surprise
You will have grown tall

Best of all, through all your life
God will always be there for you
So call on him in anything
You ever say or do

You are a special child of God
This guarantee is there forever
The baptism you will receive
Will be taken from you never

CHRISTMAS

The Christ Child was born
We celebrate each year
A candlelit service
With the story so clear

Our family gathered
Our prayers have been said
Table laden with food
Now the masses are fed

The gifts shared and opened
The great joy of giving
Then too soon to part
And go about living

With memories of sharing
That last all year through
To remind us always
Sharing every day we should do

Teaching our children
That Christ's birth was to save
Faithful Christians forever
If to sin not a slave

God granted this gift
Later gave him to perish
Takes away all our sins
A daily gift to cherish

So teaching of giving
Should start with this story
To teach them the meaning
And give God the glory

I pray you and your family have a blessed Christmas and a peaceful, healthy new year. Dk

Christmas 2011

Just a quick note to bring some updates and bore others with our crazy lives! We are still old, and that is a good thing. The alternative is not so good. The gray hair is picking up speed, and everything else is really slowing down. The hearing (or lack thereof) situation in this household leaves something to be desired. The misinterpretation problem around here could qualify for *Saturday Night Live*!

The kids and grandkids and one great-granddaughter are all great. Darren and Clay are both consultants in the oil patch, and John, Morgan's husband, is a mud engineer, so we have some knowledge of what's going on with the Eagle Ford Shale boom in DeWitt and surrounding counties. Still waiting on our ship. Tina is in her last year of coaching PE and will be retired next year, and we will have to find her an outlet for her still endless energy. Robin is still retired and keeps Kaylor (I'm the mother of a grandmother!) along with day care and subletting her to us when things get busy. Needless to say she has us all wrapped around every finger!

Morgan drives to San Antonio three days for her job. Kendall (Jake), in San Diego, changed jobs and is working for a family counselor and likes it. Jake is with a family business doing fire detectors in commercial buildings. Keary is an assistant manager in retail with AT&T, and they keep her very busy. Madi is teaching and coaching basketball in Huffman Independent School District (ISD) and really likes it there. She and Chuck are getting married in June. He is also teaching and coaching in another school district, so that should work for them. Loren is in his third year at UTSA and not playing football. (That didn't work out.) Now he can zero in on academics. Kaylor (three in February) has just participated in her third wedding this month and actually got up to the altar in this one. She took her catalogue to tell Santa what she wanted for Christmas (not a good sign). We all stay busy, don't know what we do, but we do a lot of it.

I am having my kitchen enlarged, and there is a delay with construction, which caused my appliances to be out of warranty, and they are still in the box in the garage (typical for us). We haven't traveled this year because of the fact we were waiting for builders. We will get started in January (will report on that next year).

Kermit still does his cattle, and that keeps him off the streets. He and his two dogs are a regular all over town. I still do every dog and pony show that comes along—circle, communion to nursing home, choir, bridge, canasta, to name a few. I am doing them slower, though. The kids and grandkids are trying to keep me in the know with my computer, camera, and cell phone, which really takes a toll on my brainpower.

We are thankful for all our blessings. We wish you and your families a merry Christmas and a blessed new year!

Christmas 2014

Greetings!

If it hasn't dawned on you yet, this year is very near to the end. This indicates that it is very near to Christmas, which brings us to Advent. My prayers are that this Advent season brings us all preparing for the celebration of Jesus.

This year has been very good to us in that we are all well, for which we are so grateful. Kermit and I were blessed with a trip to Ireland in June and spent our fifty-fifth anniversary there with a most wonderful group we traveled with. Shortly after our return, I had surgery in Houston, correcting an abdominal problem, which I had been dealing with most of the year to that point. Now we are both in good health "for our age."

We are planning to do U.S. trips in 2015 in view of Ebola, ISIS, and whatever will develop by the first of the year. We stay busy with family, church, museum, and library and still follow sports, local and other. We enjoy seeing old and new friends, so if you are in the area, please drop by, and the coffeepot is always on.

We were saddened by the death of Kermit's brother Lamar in December and the death of a great-great nephew on December 13, 2014.

Darren is still consulting around Bowie and ranches, hunts, and makes Spurs games now that football season is over. Tina is still retired and has really learned to enjoy it. She stays very busy with family and extended family and my personal shopper as she travels to San Antonio with both kids living there. Keary is doing athletic classes in San Antonio for homeschooled and keeps busy looking for full-time work. Loren has graduated from UTSA and is a personal trainer trying to increase his clientele.

Clay and Robin are still enjoying country life. Clay is consulting around Hallettsville, and they both enjoy fishing on their days off. Robin is always busy with house, yard, and grandchildren. They were blessed to have them all home for Thanksgiving. Robin makes frequent trips to Austin and San Diego to help with her sweet babies.

Morgan and John and Kaylor were blessed with baby sister, McKinley Hazel Carriger, on December 12 of this year and are so thankful and happy. Christmas is special to them this year. For now, Morgan is a stay-at-home mom; John, a mud engineer, works all over; and Kaylor, in kindergarten at St. Michaels School in Cuero, keeps us all busy with soccer, gym, and so on. We love it all! McKinley makes our fourth great-grandchild.

Kendall, Jake, and Reese (turned two on December 12, 2014) are happy living a busy life on the West Coast. San Diego is home for them, and they are busy with Reese, work, and travel. Jake's family owns a fire prevention company and actually have a contract for a year's work in Galveston beginning this December. Kendall works part time as office manager for a friend's family counseling practice. They enjoy skiing at Mammoth, and Jake is an avid surfer.

Madi and Chuck began school year with a new baby, new house, new campus for Madi, and new school for Chuck. Surviving this all, they are teaching and coaching, Madi at Lake Travis Middle School and Chuck at Marble Falls High School. What doesn't kill you makes you stronger is true for them. Their house is at Spicewood area of Austin. They were blessed with Tatum Marie Cook on March 3, 2014. She is a healthy, happy "gym brat" who takes it all in stride. They are very busy and get down to Yorktown when they can, and we get up there when they have an opening.

So we are happy with this small-town life with a trip here and there to see how the rest of the world functions. It's always so good to travel and so good to get back home to all our family and friends. May you all have a blessed Christmas and a happy new year!

Kermit and Doris

Christmas 2015

Just a note to fill you in
Or bring you up to date
About the year that just flew by
And why this greeting's late

Our family once again increased
Great-grandson from the West
Born to Jake and Kendall
And Reese thinks he's the best

Austinites the Cooks reside
To coach and teach each day
Then come home to Tatum
And she ready to play

Keary and Loren in San Antonio
Children of Tina and Darren
All well and working hard
Neither yet talking marrin'

Locally live Morgan and John
Kaylor and McKinley too
One in school, one at home
With always much to do

Robin and Clay the countryfolks
Work hard and then do fishing
She retired, he off just now
To get back to work he's wishing

Tina retired, Darren ranching
Waiting for job to resume
Busy as ever day in and out
Job soon coming up we assume

KC turned eighty in the fall
Doris is still thirty-nine
RV-ing travel and family
Stay busy most of the time

We are blessed as always
With health and love and living
We wish all a merry Christmas
For the past year give thanksgiving

Christmas Lights

Christmas lights will soon come down
Trees and stockings put away
One thing we can't discard
Is the Christ Child born that day

Keep the light within us
To carry through the year
Share it as you journey
With the story that's so dear

All that is promised us
Started with this birth
God sending his son
To dwell with us on earth

Knowing that his death to come
To wash away our sin
As early as his holy birth
When God's gift did begin

So light will always be
A sign of his hope for all
Every sun and moon and star
And candle glow a call

The comfort that light brings
A promise that is sure
The only way, the truth
For us the pain he bore

So Christmastime will last all year
Within our hearts so glad
Keep the divine birth in mind
And the celebration we've just had

Shout it from the rooftops
Whisper it in awe
Sing it with a glorious joy
Like the angles saw

Components of Life

All life is of God
He is the beginning and the end
All that lies between
In this life we must contend

He is with us always
Though times we abstain
His grace and peace offered
Free gifts of his divine reign

This earthly life a journey
Searching for this peace
While all the while explicit
That his promise will not cease

On his created earth we dwell
In this short time to grow
Our human preparation
Searching what is to know

Though daily lives are filled
With needs to live our days
If following his wisdom
He will guide us all our ways

Struggles, joy, and peace
A mixture in this scheme
Strengthening our souls
For the eternal heavenly scene

Always love the Lord your God
And your neighbor as would you
Live in truth and kindness
As his calling we should do

When we fall away at times
As he knows we all do
His forgiving reassurance
Will always carry through

Come What May

"Come what may"
A quote from the past
Give it some thought
"What may?" you ask

"It is what it is"
This, too, often said
A message given
Whether good or bad

So often forgotten
The wisdom of this
Still so simple and wise
A point we may miss

Volumes of references
From another time
"Just wait and see"
One that comes to mind

A wise thing to practice
Their words still apply
Our names have just changed
Though the point does comply

Coming Home

We were out of town last week
To a wedding once again
Had a lovely time to meet
And drive home through the rain!

The rain has brought a smile to folks
Preparing for the fall
Once again God saved the day
Let's thank him one and all

The grass is green and growing
The earth seems fat and sound
Soon the coastal can be cut
Again hay on the ground!

Now the rain has shown its worth
Seems more value than the oil
All is good in its own way
How precious is our soil

Constant

Every day you live
Every second, minute, hour
God is constantly present
With his all-knowing power

As we rush about our day
Thinking we are on our own
He is aware of every thought and deed
The choices ours alone

His love remains constant
Whether we call on him or not
To turn to him for guidance
An option passed a lot

Every undertaking we enter
Ask his blessing on your task
Give him then the glory
You will be so glad you ask

If a lifestyle is developed
With his presence in mind
What peace and joy is found
A promise to all humankind

But we are only human
Not perfect as our savior
We fall from grace at times
His forgiveness in our favor

Trust in this pardon
Strive to do his will
This is the divine mystery
That he will love us still

Share this word to all
As you go about your day
As one precious sous is saved
Then continue in this way

You may never see the day
When a life has come to know
The love God has for all
Plant the seed, and it will grow

Continuing Christmas

The party's over
The day of his birth
Celebration continues
Tell all the earth

Jesus was born
To save us all
Don't pack that away
With that new Christmas ball

Celebrate each day
The whole year through
In all that you say
And all that you do

Proclaim the wonder
Of the gift so great
Eternal salvation
Not greed and hate

Pass on the love
That this gift brought
To one and to all
Proclaim as we ought

Sharing the promise
Of this gift from above
So all may know
God's greatest love

May the source of your spirit
Come from this very gift
Be contagious to all
All spirits to lift

Whatever life brings
To this journey on earth
Remember the promise
And joy of this birth

Day by Day

Day by day we live
Each hour passing by
How we choose to spend them
Where our chosen path does lie

Each day a gift to cherish
So precious and so new
To honor and respect each
With all you say and do

Our lives demand attention
As all should strive to tend
The best of our abilities
As each used day will end

Past days are gone forever
Never to relive
Therein lies the secret
That our very best we give

We cannot see a future day
With faith in God we fare
Good and bad alike arise
With his strength we bear

In this complicated world
The words of God remain
Clinging to this promise
We have everything to gain

So as these days come and go
We are to do our part
Grace to strengthen hearts and minds
As each new day we start

Days in Our Lives

Each day a new story
A new tale to tell
Some just great
Some don't go well

This makes life interesting
A surprise every turn
Then some humdrum
Some days we learn

Mystery of the unknown
Awakening to take part
In whatever flows
When a new day we start

Some days we are burdened
Then the days are all peace
Our paths tend to follow
A method of release

If each day is productive
We have done what we can
Giving back to others
Thus serving God and man

Opportunities abounding
Resources to be used
Energy and services
Must not be abused

God and family first
Serve the country you love
A community of sharing
With guidance from above

Truth must be followed
The basis for good
Taught to all beings
Until trust is understood

DUTY

Duty versus options
Servitude or obligation
A range of responses
Freely or resignation

However it initiates
Irrelevant to the task
Just do it and get on
Without need to ask

The opportunities endless
To help, serve, or do
Overwhelming to minute
This left up to you

Each day a range of choices
Are cast across our way
To choose or choose not
Is how we live that day

Within reason to make judgment
To assist or to enable
Reason sometimes uncertain
To provide what's stable

The world today if filled
With chaos and much need
The field is wide open
To pick our chosen deed

With eyes and hearts open
We enter each new day
To near and far dilemmas
We can be that bright ray

Earthly Journey

What an adventure!
This time here on earth
A journey that is set
At the time of our birth

The paths that will open
Launched by status, peers, and such
The variables are endless
Each circumstance dictates much

The place of birth a factor
To whom you are born and where
Sets a tone for your journey
And the lives with whom you share

Poverty, pain, and struggle
Or plenty and a good life
Final destination revealing
And it will all be right

Wherever our journey takes us
Education, work, and live
It's striving for eternity
Giving all that's there to give

On this walk we encounter
Ways to witness in this land
Countless ways of giving
Of our hearts and minds and hands

The many, many lives that join
To make this journey theirs
We're guided when we seek
God's gift of which we're heirs

To one day end this journey
For the glorious one to come
This one will reign forever
As we gather there as one

Easter

The greatest gift ever
The Easter risen Lord
God gave his son so freely
Following scripture as accord

Not only did God sacrifice
His loving son for all
He suffered such a shameful death
Scripture's answered call

He took our sin upon himself
So we might be forgiven
And rest assured that we will
Live eternally in his heaven

Thus comes the joy at Easter
To know that we may live
For this is the greatest promise
Anyone could ever give

We are the blessed people
This promise meant for all
Our praise and glory always
For he lifts us when we fall

Easter is not over
When the day of Easter ends
We must share this glorious promise
To those who not know attend

EASTER

The crucifixion, resurrection
At Easter once again received
The gift of love and faith and grace
For eternity to be believed

God gave his son to die for us
To take away our sin
Suffered, died, arose to save
Salvation he did win

Our salvation he did earn
By suffering pain and death
A sacrifice for God and Christ
We thank with every breath

Lent, Holy Week, and Easter
We take with us each day
With thankful hearts rejoicing
The painful price he did pay

Rejoicing for the loving gift
We take with us always
With praise and adoration
Our voices then we raise

Share this news with all you meet
For some have never heard
This commission, ours for life
To spread the loving word

This precious gift for all of time
Can never be compared
With anything to ever come
For us his life not spared

Love your neighbor as yourself
A way to share God's gift
A daily way to live and die
Many spirits we could lift

End of Day

The end of the day
The sunset speaks
Tells us to cease
The horizon peaks

Time to gather
To review the day
There is tomorrow
At the sun's first ray

Consider the day
That first light brings
A whole new view
Of unknown things

Change will come
As we journey on
Accepting whatever
Comes with the dawn

Keeping in mind
God gave us this day
Ask him to guide us
What we do and say

If each day is lived
To the good of all
By every person
This is our call

So when the day ends
And we look back and see
What have I done
That will reflect me

If you are at peace
With the day past
Pass it on to all
To fulfill your task

Endurance

Have you weathered a bad storm
Have you gone the longest mile
Have you climbed the highest mountain
Have you suffered a long while

Within a normal lifetime
Some of these may come our way
How we react to such trials
Counts at the end of day

Remembering Philippians 4
The thirteenth verse does say
"I can do all things though Christ"
Will strengthen you this way

It need not be a raging storm
Long mile or mountain high
It may be a troubled time
Not understanding why

Life brings both highs and lows
Not for us to understand
Some are thrust upon us
Others by our own hand

Being humans we're not perfect
Choices made good and not
If wisdom comes with error
Over time could learn a lot

So make molehills out of mountains
Short walks, not the long mile
Gentle showers and no storms
Enjoy life all the while

Family

F is for father
Strength comes to mind
A is for those able
In families you find

M is for mother
The hub of the home
I is for inclusive
So none feels alone

L is for love
The life of the home
Y is for the years
That it takes to become

The word "family" has meaning
A unit bound by ties
No matter what number
Where loyalty abides

A precious gift, family
To cherish and treasure
The reward is amazing
Beyond any measure

Whatever your family
Numbered or small
Together with bonding
You can weather it all

FATHERS

On Father's Day we honor
All our fathers dear
In our lives today
Though some no longer here

God the eternal father
Created early man
Teaching love and grace
In ways no man can

Fathers of this earthly time
All of history have led
As a blessing in each home
Where God is the chosen head

Providing all a family needs
In early years the way
He the sole breadwinner
When the mother home did stay

Still the strength and leader
For wife and children too
Protecting and guiding
In all that families do

Respect and honor due
As sons learn a father's way
To continue paternal leadership
As they, too, father one day

As head of all the house
An example he must live
All to follow in his footsteps
A loving gift to give

A family living loved and safe
More precious than any gold
Led by fathers caring and
To the family circle hold

FATHERS

There are fathers who are wise
There are fathers who are wrong
The blessed ones know the Lord
And those blessings make them strong

What a privilege to be a father
Strong in faith and truth and love
Blessings that live forever
When seeking strength from God above

God is the greatest father
His love so great for all
He gave his only son
For forgiveness when we fall

A father who's committed
To child and spouse and home
Together build a lifestyle
With God the cornerstone

Fathers should be honored
Respected, loved, obeyed
In return his role includes
Groundwork for a child's life laid

When fathers become grandfathers
The joy that is returned
Creates another time to teach
From one's lifetime lessons learned

A grandchild's love so innocent
Deserves to be received
Returns tenfold always
A true blessing when achieved

FREE TO BE

The freedoms that we know
So precious and so dear
To cherish and to guard
That should be very clear

This freedom is divine
God sent his son for this
To die and set us free
The realization pure bliss

Each day that we live free
From death and eternity to come
Gives birth to joy and peace
To inherit God's kingdom

Our country's also free
Unlike some torn with hate
Rulers seek evil power
And control the people's fate

Our prayers should so include
For them freedom we know
That hate and greed destroyed
Freedom for them we owe

Freedom is ours to choose
It's there, a gift for all
Free to grow in life and love
And free to choose the call

We're free to laugh, to learn, and to teach
Scripture is not denied
To decline the gift of grace
Our fate we can decide

FREEDOM NEVER SO PRECIOUS

We have so enjoyed freedom
Living in this land so free
Sometimes forgetting that
This may not forever be

We come and go at ease
In this land and wherever
Dwell and travel at will
Having restrictions never

This freedom only comes about
By our troops protecting all
From enemies meaning harm
To battle answering the call

Freedom more precious now
Than ever before we find
A Christian nation we profess
Threatening our peace of mind

Our prayers for a lasting peace
Are ways we may all take part
To ask God to protect our land
A simple honest plea of heart

FRIENDS

Friendship is a blessing
We all receive
One of God's gifts
From birth perceived

The feeling of friendship
A gift of the heart
Is a natural sense
We feel from the start

To have a friend be one
We all have this need
Prospects surround us
If opportunity we heed

Some friendships come easy
Some to develop take longer
Some last forever
Lasting and stronger

Caring a component
For friendships to grow
One may surprise you
Someone you don't know

Beware and be open
To friendships that be
As long as we're living
Must be looking to see

Friends must be cherished
And truth a great part
When you grow a trust
It must come from the heart

When friendships are broken
This should be mended
Left will widen the void
If this not attended

Friends and Food

Around the time of Christmas
The time to celebrate
With friends and food and friendship
Traditions to create

The joy of Jesus's birth
That brings us all salvation
Brings the love to surface
Promise of preservation

His birth and life and death
All lived and died for us
So freely for redemption
The prophets spoke of thus

The wonder, joy, and happiness
A natural response thus
The purest form of reverence
All sacrificed for us

To take this joy and wonder
Of the promise of his birth
And realize the actual truth
And celebrate with mirth

Now from this truth we now know
We are commissioned to reach
The ones not knowing the word
These truths we are to teach

So celebrate and fellowship
This strength together build
Prayer warriors and mission
Until the world with it is filled

From My Deer Blind

The deer are already primed
To changes in this county
Along with the drought for so long
Continue to dodge being bounty

They're also cautious and alert
To sounds invading quiet
It's hard to find the food they seek
To survive and maintain their diet

Once the quiet rolling hills
Peace the country offered
Surrounded now by mighty shale
And thus the coins now offered

It will never be the same
The noise, the lights, the smell
Although wealth may accompany
The outcome yet to tell

Games

Kick the can
Marbles
Tag
Hide-and-seek
Red light, green light
Hopscotch
Jacks
Red rover
Jump rope
Tug-of-war
Antony over
May I?
Horseshoes
Dodgeball
Simon Says
Button, button
Musical chairs
Motorboat, motorboat

Gatherings

The time of year for gatherings
A special time to meet
Weddings, reunions, graduations too
Vacations, family, time to greet

Families gather once again
To catch up and share time
Connections made and memories
Picnics, parties, food to dine

Renewing friendships, laughter
Stories old and new
Keeping friendships current
Celebrating, toasting too

Airports, theme parks, beaches
Choices each do make
Free from workplace for a time
To a mountain stream or lake

Emotions of a gathering
When grads go on their way
Celebrating but anxious
Coming to that college day

Weddings join two families
A lifetime of new ties
Merging and extending
Not just two but many lives

Refreshed from lazy summer
Refueled to welcome cooler days
Bringing other chances
To celebrate in other ways

Thanksgiving, Christmas season
Are the very special ways
To gather once again with cheer
Giving thanks for these holidays

And so a year begins again
To look forward to the days
Friends and family meet again
In the coming special ways

GATHERINGS

Family gathered 'round
Oh to gaze upon
Our ever-growing clan
Each one our hearts have won

A sudden realization
Autumn years so dear
Each phase of life more precious
Our family gathered here

All ages represented
We the oldest (will remain)
Each one has a story
Include much joy, some pain

Our blessings overflowing
For health and livelihood
Our prayerful thanks we give
Giving God the glory as we should

Trials and troubles dealt with
Laughter and fun as well
None perfect understood
Get to know us you can tell

With all our faults and gifts
We accept each just as we are
Holding up all when needed
In our very midst and afar

Our members from all regions
To gather such a delight
Add varied talents to the mix
When threatened do hang tight

As families go we're average
Each designed by God's hand
To honor his creation
Do our share in this great land

Gathering Thoughts

To gather one's thoughts
One must be still
A quiet time to ponder
To think as you will

The pace of living
This day as we go
Little time for thinking
An escape some know

Planning takes thought
Projecting as well
If one doesn't focus
Results you can't tell

Stopping to think
Before any task
Be it domestic or other
Not too much to ask

Too often we plunge
Into unknown space
Not prepared to deal
Then need to save face

A little preparation
And thinking each day
Eliminates stresses
Saving time in this way

To allow this to be
A quiet place is so dear
Makes thinking happen
When the mind is clear

When much time goes by
And we rush all the day
The gift of thinking
May fall by the way

Getting Lost in the Day

Proceeding to the washer
See a plant to tend
On the way to that task
Thought of mail to send

Coming from the mailbox
Saw some weeds to pull
There out in plain sight
I saw the trash was full

Emptied trash, returned the can
And saw the grass was dry
To the faucet then I went
When fallen limbs I walked by

Picking up the fallen limbs
I saw the mail had come
Walked to get the daily mail
Took time to inspect some

Place the mail inside the house
And saw the wash not done
Placed it in the washer
And then the water run

Before I could continue
I found no soap to use
Jumped in car to go buy
Did not have time to lose

Passing by a shop in town
Saw a Huge Sale sign
Couldn't pass a chance to "save"
Although it was way past nine

Made a saving purchase
Proceeded to task at hand
Needed bread and made a stop
At grocery store did land

Made it home before too long
To take the bread inside
Decided to make a piece of toast
And did my time abide

Realized the wash not done
Took the soap and got it going
Soon time to think of lunch
When honey finished mowing

So the day continued
To dart from chore to chore
Cleaned the kitchen, folded the clothes
And then went look for more

Many tasks got started
Few completed at the time
So I'll try again tomorrow
For tomorrow, too, is mine

GETTING TO KNOW PEOPLE

What a joy to know
When we meet someone new
The chance to make a friend
Or acquaintance of a few

The gift of gab a tool
To engage in conversation
Soon a connection made
Often quite a sensation

Young and old alike
The gift of tongue used sincerely
Can bring about such comfort
Joy to some so dearly

North or south or east or east or west
People will soon respond
If one makes the first step
Possibly create a bond

Wherever you find yourself
Each day a chance to greet
Known and unknown souls
With opportunities to meet

Traveling both near and far
People of other places
Eagerly as well to seek
New names and new faces

Chances are you will never see
This person ever again
The one impression you may make
A memory they will sustain

Take every opportunity
To engage in friendly talk
You will be surprised to find
It also brings joy to your faith walk

GIVING BACK

Have you ever discovered
When you render aid
The reward is not in giving
But a new freedom you have made

Large sums need not be involved
Or vigorous actions done
A simple thoughtful pleasure
For you and the assisted one

Literally a helping hand
When seeing the true need
Is just as precious a gesture
As the most gallant deed

Awareness is the key to know
When response in needed
Done in love for man or beast
Appropriately heeded

All around us every day
Opportunities abound
From small to major aid
Us continually surround

Tact and honest caring
Important in this giving
Maintaining one's dignity
Regardless of ways of living

Done quietly and private
Most often the best choice
To maintain pride for others
No need to have a voice

This giving is God's teaching
The joy that comes with sharing
"Love your neighbor as yourself"
Is the truest way of caring

GIVING THANKS

God of love and grace and healing
I come on bended knee
Humbly giving thanks
For the loving gift from thee

The short trial I endured
Raised prayers as trials do
You heard our prayers as always
Granting a miracle from you

Surrounded by your presence
Gave assurance you were there
The answer to our prayers
Shows your constant loving care

May I keep this gracious sign
To witness to your glory
By sharing always your love
In this my grateful story

The promise of your caring
And with constant prayer and praise
Raised in true obedience
Help me witness all my days

Thanks to family, friends, and fellowship
Surrounded by your caring
Overwhelmed I also give you thanks
You helped my burden bearing

God's Earth

"For the beauty of the earth"
The song says it so true
Our earth is beauty in itself
Undone by what man will do

Our greatest treasure, hope, and home
God created it just for man
We've slowly done disservice
Challenged, restore, preserve we can

The springtime growth tells us
That our good earth will still provide
But if we continue the abuse
Be certain abundance will subside

Rampant use of nature's gifts
Without thought of days to come
Will soon turn our world into
A barren place, undone

Unnatural elements that harm
The nature of our earth
Brought to immediate attention
Before we lose its worth

Each individual is challenged
To do their personal part
Strive for improvement
And reclaiming earth will start

Going Home

His earthly journey ended
God's heavenly peace now known
He walks among the saints
His final battle won

The glimpse he had of heaven
Prepared him for the end
He shared, assured his people
So with peace they now may send

He walks with God in heaven
Healed and whole and saved
Take comfort in the promise
His path with gold is paved

Good Things

Good things are so simple
Like sunshine and the rain
Clean, cool water to drink
A tree-lined, shady lane

Just take a look around you
Really good things are free
A meadow of wildflowers
Autumn leaves down from a tree

Dew on a web in the morning
A bird on a windowsill
A butterfly darting about
A tiny rabbit so soft and still

Fresh churned butter to eat
A loaf of fresh baked bread
A family around the table
Clean sheets on your fresh made bed

The smell of fresh mowed grass
Or a field of fresh cut hay
The smell of rain from a shower
A sunset at the end of day

A timid fawn discovered
The breeze of a cool fall day
Geese flying toward the south
Baby kittens sweet at play

A newborn baby's gaze
The wonder of their birth
A rocking chair by a window
To know peace and its worth

A hot steaming cup of coffee
The sun's rays through a cloud
A field of untouched snow
Dad at son's game so proud

A rooster's crowing in the morning
See a barn from days gone by
A cow grazing in a meadow
The scent of a fresh baked pie

There is good and beauty around us
If only we look to see
Mostly good and so subtle
It is what it is to be

Greetings from Koehler's Korner

It's December 14, 2015. This year has passed so quickly it's almost impossible to recall all of it. Once again our blessings outweigh everything else. Everyone is working or going to school, except for Kermit and me; we just follow everyone's lives the best we can.

Tina and Robin are retired but work harder than ever. Darren and Clay are still consulting. Morgan and John lost their twin girls this August, a sadness we are all trying to understand. Kaylor is doing well in pre-K at St. Michael's school in Cuero. Kendall and Jake and Reese visit Texas several times a year. Reese turned one on December 12, and some of us went out to San Diego to help her celebrate. Keary made a career change and works in San Antonio three days a week and two days at our church's new learning garden and seems to love what she is doing. Madi and Chuck relocated to Lake Travis ISD in Austin and love the whole move. They are expecting little Tatum (girl) in February. Loren is at UTSA, finishing this May doing the "Tough Mudder" events every chance he gets (an endurance course you pay to do with the proceeds going to help wounded warriors).

Kermit and I had the privilege of touring Scotland this August, which was a really good trip. In September we went to Munich for their Octoberfest, which was a fun time. We are still resting up from that.

Keeping up with the events of all concerned keeps us in the know; we just don't remember much of it! Robin and Clay fish often and keep us in fresh fish. Several of us hunt, and Darren and Kermit have gotten their bucks. Doris missed hers still time.

Kermit and Darren have cattle together, and that keeps them busy. Kermit does what he can, and Darren stays very busy on his "days off."

I am still addicted to baking, and our new kitchen sure makes that a greater joy. I still do some church work and help with Kaylor when they can catch me.

Our intention in 2014 is to do more RV-ing. We have missed that since our group is falling by the wayside health wise and can't get the gang together.

We wish you all a blessed Christmas and a healthy, happy new year! Keep in touch, and when you're in the area, stop by, and let us bore you some more!

If we have failed to acknowledge a wedding, a birthday, an anniversary, a funeral, a divorce, please forgive us—our memory isn't what it used to be.

Love from Crestview, Yorktown, and Texas

Greeting the New Day

When you awake each morning
Refreshed with restful sleep
A quiet time to meditate
Before a busy day you meet

It's here where you decide
How you're to live this day
Begin with a quiet prayer and praise
Overcoming come what may

This is the "ideal" morning
Which does not always come
Schedules, interruptions, whatever
Until the day is done

As the day progresses
A moment will arise
When a thought of song or scripture
Produces a peaceful surprise

Make up your mind each morning
This day the Lord has blessed
Do your best with all that is
Drawn from your night of rest

Some days bring joy or sorrow
Accepting this is what you do
Draw strength from God's grace
Promised each morn for you

As long as we journey here
A morning dawns anew
Just as sure as the sun comes up
A fresh new day for you

Grief, Sorrow, and Pain

What a wonder this life to live
A privilege and honor each day
A challenge, a journey, a mystery
Just meet and greet what may

Some journeys are filled with joy
Some grief, sorrow, and pain
My prayer is that whatever the case
Our efforts will not be in vain

To share the pain, joy, and efforts
Of each soul that passes our way
Is the commission the Lord gives us
An honor we must share every day

HEARTS

A beating heart
The source of all living
So taken for granted
The lifeblood it is giving

The heart of a family
Held together with love
Providing a haven
God sent from above

The heart of a country
A central place of command
Directing each region
With a responsible hand

The heart of a sweetheart
The heart found in a mate
The heart of a parent
A heart destroys hate

A heart filled with love
As God had for us all
That he sent us his son
To have heart is our call

HE IS RISEN!

Lilies with their trumpets sound
Easter bonnets on display
Springtime garments newly donned
To celebrate this day

Families gathered eagerly
Celebration in the air
Church bells tolling the call
Message prepared with care

What is all this eagerness
And joy within our soul
Christ has risen from the dead
This plan of God's foretold

Christ is risen, yes, indeed
Sing praises to his name
Celebrate the saving grace
The very reason Christ came

Our salvation, God's greatest gift
With grateful voices raise
Songs of saving grace and love
Thankfully, humbly praise

When we gather on this day
To thank and pray and sing
In leaving taking with us
Sharing this news we bring

God's plan is for all to know
About this gift, his son
He gave for all salvation
So every soul is won

Hi Yourself!

So excited to get a letter! I think you and I are two of the last people who write letters. I so love to get them and write them. Sorry it has taken me so long to answer, but it seems like I can't get to PC and remain long enough to finish anything.

The bougainvillea (did you know how to spell that?) is huge. What kind of soil do you have in that bed? They do OK here in sand and sun, but that is deep South Texas looking.

Sounds like your family is growing as is ours. We are expecting another great in February. Madi and Chuck (teaching and coaching in Lake Travis ISD) are expecting their first. They just made the move from humble, so new house, new job, new baby will be a lot to deal with this coming year.

Don't see Pat much, but Judy and Kraege hear from her some. She is still mad, and she emails some to keep us informed about David and her progress. I can't believe Harvey is gone, he of all of us, who enjoyed life so much. He always got us going on the class reunions, and now I will have to step up and try to keep it up.

HOME

Home means many things
A memory or a thought
A feeling you take with you
A certain scent you caught

Home remains in your heart
And always in your mind
Not ever to be erased
When absent you will find

A structure once occupied
Where nurtured, provided for
The bond established there
That made you who you are

No matter how far you go
In distance or in mind
The need to reconnect
Remains till end of time

This blessing and sweet privilege
A gift to cherish always
As you journey down life's road
And savor in later days

Take heed to create
A home to gift your heirs
This most precious inheritance
Remains forever theirs

HOME

Do you feel the sheer delight
When you arrive at home
A familiar comfort greets
Whether there is family or you alone

The homing instinct guides you
It draws you to this place
To this home you go to live
A comfort that's your base

Be it a palace or a hovel
This place belongs to you
When you return and resume
To continue things you do

A gathering of things to live
Surround your every day
Cherish this, a blessing
For some it's not that way

A routine way to function
This may draw you too
Joys and sorrows happen
In living it's what you do

A mix of work and pleasure
Maintains this way of life
Discipline helps create this
Negligence will end in strife

The mix of hope and memories
A valued part of peace
Count these an extra blessing
Makes sadness, worry cease

So when home comes in view
And you feel this surge of good
Give thanks to God for it all
Make this a practice if you would

Make a point to observe others
Whose homes have not the same
Do what is in your power
Share the hope from where you came

Pray for all homes in this world
That God's part of their days
Of the lives residing there
And guiding all their ways

HONOR

Honor, high esteem, respect
Achievements we all seek
Admiration, a product of
When of us others speak

Honor rolls and honor grads
A wall of honor for our troops
Those who gave their lives
Highest honors for our elite groups

The Pulitzer Prize an honor
Of high esteem in excellence
A worldwide distinction of greatness
A rewarding show of competence

Honorable mention as well
An honor for doing great
Along with top honors
Accomplishments considered top rate

"On your honor" a statement
Said to honor trust
The highest expression of honor
Held in high esteem you must

Honoring a special occasion
A bride, a birth, a promotion
Anniversaries, birthdays, elections
Celebrations and sharing emotions

Dishonor, a negative term
We should avoid to acquire
Earned in spite of reason
Rather than one would admire

Honor being our saving grace
Ourselves our nation all
Standing tall and honorable
It's up us to make that call

How Will We Fare

A world beyond the Eagle Ford
Away from this small place
Lives are being lived as they were
A slow and normal pace

This, too, will pass this hectic time
Would we say good or bad
The only constant being change
(Good times are being had)

The business of the world today
Ours, just a small, small, part
Time passes as will this
This obvious from the start

Overwhelming population growth
With much construction taking place
Never to be quite the same
Same town with a new face

The lights, the trucks, the traffic
A change for this quiet town
With positive growth potential
Our locals will astound

So interesting how this plays out
When all is said and done
Will we grow and prosper
Or go back to square one

With pride and positive planning
Our town could be a place
Where people care to remain
To make Yorktown their home base

Idealism

Idealism strived for
Very seldom achieved
We not being perfect
A goal hard to perceive

The pinnacle of excellence
Good to lend strength
To an attainable cause
This instructed at length

When pursuing achievements
And one's best is done well
This is the launching
A desire to excel

Excelling has levels
In all levels of call
Blending talents diverse
Exercised by most all

The world isn't perfect
But a spirit of worth
Strives for rising above
Thus driving us forth

Doing our best
In whatever we pursue
Always honestly achieving
Is the best we can do

Believing in self
And a true desire
Will bring about good
For this we aspire

Encouragement lent
Is a strengthening tool
Giving positive views
Gaining force as a rule

If You Had Journaled

Just think if you had journaled
From the very early days
How interesting to recall
How you have changed your ways

Hindsight is so very good
To second-guess some choices
In those that you made in haste
Failing to heed wise voices

All daily entries would not be
Regrets or things that you'd change
A journal just an honest script
To cover the whole range

The joyful times, the funny times
Are the most likely favored
Mingled with unlikely times
Is what makes life flavored

Take the time to think of things
That are significantly pleasing
Those being special times
Bringing joy at adult reasoning

To go back in time reliving
Forgotten times that faded
Opens minds and times past
Thus a living history if dated

Keeping entries to pass on
A legacy to those who remain
A lovely way to share your life
And for the next generation gain

Entries including births and deaths
Would be such a helpful aid
In later years to help kin
When genealogy charts are made

IMPRESSIONS

Make a good impression
What a relative term
A social requirement
Etiquette does affirm

Ingrained in our development
Our parents did so enforce
Lest we fail our peers
Email post a reliable source

Now none of us is perfect
We try to do our best
Impressions should be honest
Occasionally put you to a test

To some it doesn't matter
You may think what you may
A lesson in human nature
When one's impressions go astray

Consistent in your manner
A quote that you should heed
"Not your business what one thinks of you"
A comforting thought indeed

Some seeking wrong impressions
Matters not what you do
No two people with same opinions
That is up to you

Impressions may long linger
Or soon dismissed for good
A true and real impression
Not what others should not or should

Inez Hahn

Though the light of her eyes grows dim
The sweet smile on her face remains
While awaiting the grace of heaven
And eternal life with God she now gains

Leaving this life with assurance
Of the promise of eternal rest
Granting comfort to ones remaining
And forever share what is best

Inside a Family

Have you ever taken time to think
Beyond lives not your own
The workings of some families
And diversities not known

A soldier's family left behind
As he is called to serve
Separation, worry, loneliness
Give thanks that they deserve

A single parent trying hard
To be both mom and dad
With endless demands arising
Using all the energy one had

A couple both with corporate jobs
Demanding time and skill
With children needing said parents
All these requests must fill

A family with several children
A stay-at-home mom to all
Handling the home with skill
This being her given call

An aging retired couple
With much free time to spare
Living miles away from children
May gain joy giving others care

Jason's Journey

12-06-2018

When we wake up each morning
Dreading to start our chores
Selfishly forgetting
You would love that these be yours

But then we see your bracelet
Jason's journey Psalm 14:3
Prayers for you throughout the day
Put our hearts where they should be

So be assured we love and pray
That at your journey's ending, cured
We may then all give thanks
Commending you for what you've endured

Now give thought to power of prayer
Many voices lifting up your name
God is good and hears our plea
To heal is too his aim

JOY

Joy of the heart
Is joy of the Lord
To share with all
Is not that hard

When joy spills over
Someone will gain
The extra joy
Shared in your name

Joy is contagious
You can get or give
There's no prevention
And necessary to live

A cure for sadness
Loneliness and grief
Prevents illness
And promotes belief

Cost-free and easy
Ready to use
Works on anyone
No way to abuse

It lifts the spirit
It spreads like butter
Good for the soul
And any other

Love, grace, and joy
Go hand in hand with good
Try it, you may like it
Keep always if you could

Joy takes you through dark
When times are not great
Draw from the memory kept
And fear not for your fate

Share joy in the morning
Share joy at night
And all day long
It feels so right

It never wears out
It can never be lost
It's there hidden somewhere
To use, not to toss

Joy to the Bone

Real joy oft not recognized
Superficial joy overrated
A sense of God's true joy
Cannot be imitated

There's joy, and then there's *joy*
So real, it's to the bone
Though times of strife may come
Real joy, still, when one's alone

The sense of beyond this time
Where joy will always be
Looking at the forever
Joy in you for all to see
.

When we call on God's joy
That scripture clearly tells
That is the joy I speak of
So deep, makes true hearts swell

A joy that's overwhelming
That saturated your being
So precious that you hold it
A glow others are seeing

Just Being There

When the time comes
Whatever the need
Just being there
Is a comfort indeed

When the time comes
A joyous occasion
Just being there
To share the elation

When the time comes
To share someone's grief
Just being there
Can bring much relief

When the time comes
To help someone ill
Just being there
Can a need soon fill

When the time comes
Loneliness to share
Just being there
Makes it easier to bear

When the time comes
That a lost one returns
Just being there
Fulfill what he yearns

When the time comes
When one achieves good
Just being there
Sharing as you would

When the time comes
That one searches for peace
Just being there
You can be that release

Just for Today

Just for today
I will do my best
Having done so
Pray God does the rest

My feet though guided
Misstep along the way
My hands quite willing
Fail duty each day

My eyes and ears
Also God's gift
Not always accurate
Sight and hearing adrift

Next is my mouth
Used wisely a blessing
Falsehoods and slander
This requires addressing

The body and spirit
Attended each day
By God's tender care
Let me follow his way

When failing to do so
He forgives each wrong
Inviting obedience
With a love ever strong

So just for today
He always does his best
A teaching so simple
If I would do the rest

God, give me the wisdom
Pleasing you is my goal
Your patience and love
Will one day make me whole

Just Imagine...

No morning sun
No moon at night
No rain or wind
No dark or light

No ocean depths
Or mountain heights
No valleys green
Or distant sights

Imagine no thunder
With lightning flash
O pelting rain
Or stormy clash

No grass growing
Or trees for shade
Sweetness of flowers
Or stream to wade

No man or beast
Or living souls
Birds of the air
No warm or colds

No right or wrong
Or up or down
No yes or no
No smile or frown

No work or play
No friend or foe
No joy or grief
No stop or go

We don't have to imagine
These don't exist
God created all
This just a short list
Just imagine

Kaylor at Seven

Seven years just flew by
Now to first grade you go
Such a joy to see you learn
Few things you didn't know

You are a delight to watch
The things you love and do
Rocks and feathers also leaves
In your pocket to name a few

How you love your mom and dad
And little sister easy to see
And all cousins and your friends
Make you happy as you can be

Stay happy as you are just now
And never lose your charm
Being born on President's Day
You could take this country by storm

Keeping Christ in Christmas

Prophesy told us
That a savior be born
Sent to save us
On that Christmas morn

Never before
And never will be
An event this divine
Will life ever see

This was God's plan
To allow salvation
Such a love never known
To remove trepidation

Giving honor to God
For this awesome good
Sending his son to teach
Dying for us he would

We've taken this gift
And abused it each day
Celebrating his birth
In a most selfish way

Teaching this story
Is the utmost gift
We can give to all
Use his love to uplift

We must keep Christ in Christmas
With this lost so are
This a challenge to you
And a challenge to me

So light the candles
Sing hymns of praise
To glory in the highest
Our voices must raise

Be not afraid to commit
To a savior with pride
When the devil appears
This we must not abide

Keeping the Faith

In these times of trials
When trust is lost to some
Only by the grace of God
This battle can be won

Just mere people we profess
What can I do to heal
We can all call out to God
The only one with which to deal

Greed and power seem to grow
As did in days of old
Not until world leaders learn
With God will peace unfold

Sin will always be a choice
Our commission is to live
Such a role God did intend
A gift each of us can give

So there then is really something
That each of us can do
Keep our faith to overcome
A privilege for me and you

Our prayers to God are always heard
God knows our many needs
Granting grace to you and yours
With gifts of word and deeds

Trust in God and honor him
Regardless of what is
Profess him always to all the world
We will be eternally his

Keeping up Appearances

Keeping up appearances
A comedy of errors
Climbing the social ladder
Creates a life of terrors

"To make the grade" a challenge
To keep the position current
A struggle day by day
A liking to subservant

Needs and wants and wishes
Fantasies, desires reign
Consumes a life completely
With nothing more to gain

Real appearances matter
These not envied but admired
This message sent to imitate
Not unreal trends desired

Simplicity not a choice for all
Some choose flair and fun
A lifestyle suits one's nature
And serves both old and young

So in this journey here on earth
Accept one's style as theirs
Embrace the person, not the style
It's the embracing for which one cares

If someone in your midst admires
Appearance and the need
Graciously receive their way
And sensitivities do heed

Kermit's Eightieth Birthday

Today is your birthday
You've lived eighty years of life
Over fifty years of marriage
With your first-ever wife

The names you own are many
Like "Honey" by just me
"Dad" by our children
And "Popo" by a few

Four generations celebrate
Your special natal day
The head of all our family
There for us in every way

You've provided for us all our needs
Taught work ethics by example
Enabling all to function well
Providing lifestyles that are ample

As we continue family life
This journey we all share
God will continue blessing us
And keep us in his care

LABOR DAY

What labor means to some
When others have no clue
The span of this conclusion
Is a debate that's not new

History tells of walks of life
Where some serve and some receive
This is the way of humankind
Observance makes you believe

Work ethic a strong trait was taught
To be lazy was a sin
We have allowed this trait to fail
Success that will not win

Education, training, guidance
Are taught to equip workforces
Ethics, logic must be instilled
As well to round out the sources

"Train up a child," a mighty quote
To serve them all their days
A noble gift to give a child
To begin unselfish ways

If all able would do their share
This world would have no hunger
All would food and shelter have
And homeless would be no longer

Greed, evil, and unfairness
Have caused unbalanced living
Helpless poor hard to rise up
Not receiving help we try giving

Another area of prayer time
This problem that is raging
In this time of plenty
Our leaders should be engaging

LARS

Happiness across the way
Lars has such precious smiles
To get a text or video
Enjoyed across the miles

To share his growth and gains
And feel love from afar
A special treat to visit
Our families' new shining star

Charles IV

Another great grand came around
Joining Madi and Chuck number three
As he was now to be the fourth
Tatum, now big sister to be

C IV is of a curious mind
Exploring at every turn
Adventurous and social
Curious for all to learn

LEAVING THIS WORLD

The end of a time
When you pass from here
A joyous arrival
As was promised so dear

Those left behind
To adjust anew
A transitional time
With a whole new view

The cycle of life
Since creations start
It's a call we know
And we play our part

The big picture in mind
Helps understand this way
Live life to the fullest
Enjoying day by day

When called home
Be it young or aged
This a time to grieve
Though they be saved

Rejoicing is hard
When the pain so strong
God understands our grief
Not as a wrong

We leave pain behind
When we join again
And time is erased
However long it's been

So the promise he gave us
Can be counted on
Only needs acceptance
And we will join the throng

LIFE

The flow of life
Such a relative term
No two lives the same
Just observe and learn

Such variable options
From conception till death
What a wonderful thing
From the very first breath

Location and economics
Cultures and race
Scientific persuasion
Or accepting God's grace

What a wonderful world
We are so blessed to be
Sharing fellowship freely
Or choose not to see

Circumstances quite often
Play a big part
Navigating a path
And where life will start

Some at the mercy
Others blessed with support
Yet the outcome surprises
The ingredient, great effort

From local to worldly
Each day we make choices
Be a part of the beauty
And hear all voices

What an adventure
To watch and to be
Advantaged to participate
In this great world we see

LIFE IS A PUZZLE

Life is a puzzle
As well as are we
All consists of pieces
As different as can be

Alone a piece is partial
Part of a whole incomplete
With all parts combined
A whole unit becomes elite

Now we are whole and complete
All God intended us to be
But to be a part of society
A puzzle piece you and me

To function within life
And flow with harmony
All pieces are needed
With wisdom, this you will see

As years go by so quickly
And the puzzles of life appear
We soon recognize needed pieces
And the picture becomes clear

When you see a lone puzzle piece
And see they cannot fit with ease
Reach out and guide their way
And this effort never cease

Who wants to belong to a puzzle
With parts missing in the whole
Join hands with missing pieces
You may have saved a soul

LITTLE THINGS

Little things like dewdrops
That sparkle from the sun
A rock smooth from tumbling
Down a long, long river run

A cardinal's bright red feather
Lying in the grass so green
To find a four-leaf clover
So very seldom seen

A sudden joyful feeling
From a recalled precious time
A missing item so long searched for
Walk a forest of scented pine

The smell of baking bread
A rose that blooms all year
A soft, warm sweater
Knitted by someone dear

The sound of rain upon the roof
A nice nap in your chair
A good book shared by a friend
Funnel cakes at the fair

A greeting card in the mail
Fun snapshots of a past time
Surprises on your birthday
Finding two words that will rhyme

A friendly pat on the shoulder
A hug when you feel down
Laughing children playing
A smile to erase a frown

All these things seem little
And there are so many more
Think through your yesterday
The little things we all store

LOVE THY NEIGHBOR

Who is my neighbor
It is easy to see
If you will look around
So near they may be

Your neighbor is anyone
You encounter each day
Treat them with love
By what you do and say

A neighbor may be next door
Or a hundred miles away
Every opportunity presented
With much respect do pay

Another city is a neighbor
Which you join in harmony
Another state deserves the same
As good neighbors we should be

Nations as well are neighbors
The logistics should be met
To do the best for all concerned
With international love then met

How lovely would this finally be
If indeed we lived this out
With every kind word and deed
What God's love is all about

May it start with you and me
And spread this love around
Teaching simple kindnesses
Peace and joy may then be found

Prayers for all neighbors
Would be heard by God above
We can plead our need for peace
That would fill all hearts with love

MATURING

Oh, the joy, maturity
Carefree as days go by
Carefree to visit doctors
For our prescription "high"

No longer gainfully employed
The "rainy day" we'd so await
Now it's here so very soon
To greet our senior fate

Chores take longer to complete
Naps twice a day required
Now food and drinks are limited
Can't eat as once desired

Children and grandchildren
The highlight of our days
The joy they add to life
In so many loving ways

When evening comes each day
Bedtime is a treat
Whenever so tired, we retired
To find, we cannot sleep

Social function such a must
Each one we did attend
And now it's a delight
When no invites, don't offend

All in all it's such a delight
To age together all these years
Still learning to give and to take
As our "autumn" time appears

McKinley

Here she comes
Ready or not
Makes herself known
With the smile she's got

Her sweet nature lasts
As long as she knows
You'll grant her wish
And "her way" all goes

An inquisitive nature
She knows her mind
Loves hugs and kisses
A happier kid you'll not find

MEMORIES

Around the table talking
After delicious food and drink
When all are mellow and relaxed
Of memories we think

Stories, laughter, tales are told
Each thought a story brings
Soon the table fills again
With love, fellowship, precious things

Childhood days relived with glee
A different slant from whom told
Depending on who has the floor
Retelling stories of old

Forefathers' stories oft recalled
Discovering traits repeated
Only then are all aware
Some better left deleted

Memories aren't all ideal
Lives aren't lived like this
Honest talk, loving support
Are gifts we should not miss

Family we will always be
No matter where and when
In the end, when gathered 'round
A table love will all mend

So to the table your life bring
To share what we all are
Exciting, boring, whatever is
We bring from near and far

Share your stories, everyone
Heritage for all to know
Keep them alive and don't deny
The next age to share it so

Morning

In the quiet of the morning
When the earth is not awake
The stillness such a wonder
And a peacefulness does make

Before the sun approaches
To dry the morning dew
Nocturnals seeking prey
With quiet nighttime view

When rays from morning sun
Light the world's new day
Birds of feather to awake
Offering songs their sweet way

As creatures begin to scurry
The warm sun does them awake
To forage in the grass and fields
For the day food to partake

This morning scene we often miss
When outdoors we fail to share
Sharing nature's awesome beauty
God created with such care

Speaking of God's creation
Taking place since day one
Each daily need still providing
When another day is done

Mothers

Though your mommas told you this
But now I put to rhyme
All the worthy things we learn
We will pass on in time

Glue holds not a candle
To the strength of a fierce mother
Her grit and grip hold better
With a loyalty like none other

And this same mother nurtures
With tender loving care
The cherished ones defended
Yet treating each one fair

The role of mothers varies
Each day a new hat wears
Laboring for each member
Showing that she cares

Blessings that you gain from her
With no need for thanks or praise
Given with unselfish love
Enough for all to raise

Moms have a force of nature
Which God did so design
Scripture giving guidelines
Withstanding for all time

Beyond the day of we honor
With family gathered 'round
Remember daily thanking
For love and strength she's found

Mothers

Mothers of the world
Oh, where to begin
A word so broad
Scarce to take in

Blessed with mothers
And we all were
Giving us life
God's blessing to her

A life-changing blessing
When self is on task
A lifelong commitment
Newborns did not ask

The love of a mother
Second only to the Lord
A fierce protection
Before cutting the cord

This life presented
Fulfilling sweet dreams
A guiding task
Carried out by all means

This bond isn't broken
By absence or such
Love of the heart
Has a lingering touch

The heart of the home
To direct and nurture
Making family work
A child gains a future

In memory or living
A mother is always
Cherish her kindly
Today and all days

MOVING FORWARD

"You must move forward"
Words you cannot hear
After loss of something
You've held very dear

Moving forward from a point
When sadness helps to mask
Fears and doubts of self
And recovery quite a task

Through life lessons, not failure
Reality helps one grow
Disappointments, joys experienced
Teaching wisdom you only know

Avoid adding baggage
Release that heavy load
How lightly becomes travel
To enjoy life's embracing road

Yearn not for perfection
This world will never give
Seek peace and joy through wisdom
As you journey forward to live

"Ideal" is seldom realized
Waste no precious time for this
To insist only brings you grief
While the healing thing you miss

Moving forward a personal task
Customized for just your pace
God is with you every step
Be strong, accept his grace

My Kitchen Window

Outside my kitchen window
Such a sight to see
Flowers, grass, and birds
The green leaves of a tree

How blessed I've been to savor
This peaceful scene each day
Not the scene of wars' destruction
As in places far away

To see green trees and not destruction
Of homes and all the land
To live in hope and peace
For us by God's kind hand

To understand this contrast
Is not for us to be
Why wars are waged forever
Deciding who lives free

The blessing of our free birth
In this our great land
Is something we fail to grasp
All through God's gracious hand

Our prayers for other war-torn lands
Where people don't live free
Is our commission one and all
For the freedom they should see

So when we view our countryside
Even though it's dry
We have so very much that's good
All this our whole lives, why

Never, never take for granted
Troops have paid a mighty price
To keep us free to see the green
    At a mighty sacrifice

When you look out your window
Say, "Thank you, Lord, for this"
When you see an enlisted one
Thank them for our lives of bliss

Mysteries of Life

Oh, the mysteries of life
Man thinks he must discover
If one knew all mysteries
What would be to recover

Some things should continue
A mystery remaining
To wonder and ponder
Some never obtaining

If all were revealed
What would be left to find
We are not intended
To have all this in mind

What lengths man will go
And dangers do meet
To unearth mysteries
Some ending in defeat

When mysteries emerge
By their own surrender
Released by God's will
Not by man's agenda

Mysteries solved
That survived in the past
Now solved and learned
New ones emerge to last

The developing world
With new mysteries and old
Continue to tempt man
To be curious and bold

NEIGHBORS

Love your neighbor as yourself
What is this verse to me
We ask who would this include
All in the world told he

Some neighbors come and go
Some remain for all time
It matters not the story
This love must thus be mine

In daily life a neighbor
Comes in diverse persons
What you alone make of this
Are some of many versions

Treat your neighbor as yourself
The return may not be mutual
Love them and treat them in spite
Though reciprocating is futile

Many live harmonious
When living this commandment
How peacefully would neighbors dwell
In sincere, loving abandonment

Now this ideal way of living
Without human-devised style
Only perfect through divinity
Living in harmony all the while

Man not perfect or divine
Flaws in our daily living
Neighbors experience this as well
Thus creates a time for giving

Worldly neighbors, too, are we
To lands far and wide
Now is the time to pray for peace
And his commandment abide

NEW LITTLE ANGELS

The poem I write today
Is not for usual cheer
In view of recent grief
For the slain children dear

I ask one and all
And I know you do
Lift them up in prayer
For our society too

Words cannot comfort now
No matter what we say
As time passes oh so slowly
Pray some hurt will go away

All the children sweet and dear
Are with God and good
But the earthly void remains
Sharing their pain we would

The ripples of this travesty
So far they spread to all
Striking fear to all young hearts
So sad for ones so small

For days ahead we must pray
Families will suffer long
Keep them in our thoughts and prayers
Though will not ease the wrong

Angels fitted in halos and wings
And their eternal home is won
Though parents want them back
They are rejoicing with the saving one

Understanding this will never be
While we dwell in this life
But when we all unite again
There will remain no strife

OBSERVATIONS

Sharing a smile
Eye contact
The gentle touch
A kindly act

Observe these gifts
And see their worth
A spirit lifted
A hint of mirth

Small effort spent
To choose to please
When sure response
Comes with such ease

Detecting needs
Easily observed
Approach emphatically
With honesty deserved

What joy resulting
Giving and received
A glad spirit lifted
A downhearted relieved

To be remembered
A gift of time
A precious act
Of yours or mine

A loving deed
To pass along
Seen and felt
To help grow strong

Observation, Obligation, Obedience

Observation, a powerful gift
To see and know and heed
Leading to one's surroundings
Aware of a special need

Obligation to react positively
As second nature's way
Take on the need as yours
And practice day by day

Obedience follows closely
Without, nothing better gained
Execute the needed aid
Prevent a spirit maimed

These ideals followed closely
Some not to be obtained
Only our best foot forward
Best intentions are ordained

With prayer and God's blessings
Go about with all zeal
Like it is all up to you
And pray it's his to heal

Prayerful needs surround us
Opportunities abound
The Holy Spirit leading us
The outcomes will astound

Divinity at our disposal
Ask and he will hear
Leading us to service
He is really just that near

Hope your week was another of good things or at least tolerable at best. (They can't all be the greatest.) Ours was busy as usual. Went to Huffman to see Madi coach her first basketball game and saw her classroom. She won her game and seems like her classes are going well also. Pray for rain and all our ill and grieving and especially our country. Thanks for all of our blessings. Doris 3-16-13

Oh, the Joy Remaining

In these troubled times
There's much joy to be had
Though chaos is embraced
The world is not all bad

The love of God is constant
In spite of Satan's plan
God is here for you and me
For this then we must stand

Focus on the beauty
This world still holds for all
Deny evil temptations
God's power is Satan's fall

The joy of good lives that we know
Must be our pledge to keep
Never give way to Satan's call
That will only sorrow reap

The beauty of our families
Of home and church and good
The country that we dwell in
For all this God has stood

Stick to God's salvation plan
The cross and promise true
What more joy can we ask
That only God can do

Teaching the lessons taught us
To young and old alike
This the only way to reach
To find our eternal height

OLD SELF, NEW YEAR

Tucking 2014 away
Welcome to the new year
The year 2015 has arrived
So very glad we're here

Renewing promises of change
Thinking to improve one's self
Let's be honest and OK
Without power, fame, or wealth

All the past years now recalled
Look back and glean the good
Leave behind the negative
Wouldn't change if you could

Reflect, reminisce, renew
And go with what you've learned
The old self is not so bad
Forget some things once yearned

Looking forward to the new year
And whatever it may bring
After all what choice have we
But with grace and prayer to cling

If per chance we could view
The future of this year
We would be wary to begin
Knowing the things to fear

So let's all just live as good
As we are able with God's love
Do as we should on this earth
With God's guidance from above

One Day at a Time

In all that we do
Within our own will
We've only so much time
In a day which to fill

Routines of the day
Done without thought
It's the things added on
Sometimes more than we ought

Careful thought would be good
At this time as we plan
Beyond our endurance
Schedule more than we can

The thing to remember
As we stress being behind
Think of things that matter
Take one day at a time

Common sense should be
Our guide at this phase
Doing what we're able
In all of our days

Enjoying what you do
Is the secret of peace
Learn this and pursue it
Bringing joy without cease

This joy-bringing spirit
That inspires your task
Making days flow smoothly
In your accomplishment bask

Open Hands

Giving or receiving
Open hands an indication
A sign of intention
Of giving, dedication

Open hands so generous
Versus closed fist showing
A visual of nongiving
Showing thoughts so knowing

A sign of stress or anger
This fist we make so fast
Recognized so often
An impression makes to last

Hands a tool of persons
Used to give or take
A loving heart's hands
Are open, gifts to make

Hands that cradle children
Create a comfort zone
Remaining with us always
As few others to us known

A sincere handshake given
Will seal a friendship swift
Continuing to serve you
And give a heart a lift

Hands serve as a lesson
Remember Jesus's they did pierce
To give us our salvation
With that sacrifice so fierce

Using your hands wisely
Will always serve you well
Reaching out with open hands
Can a loving gesture tell

OUR LOVE

I'll love you till the day I die
And love you long thereafter
May nothing ever change this love
Of joy and tears and laughter

Discoveries we early found
So precious then and now
Recalling when we celebrate
The day we took this vow

The years of building a life
The plans, the work, the fun
Two awesome children then
Bringing joy compared with none

The years of living our life
Bringing usual ups and downs
God saw us through this all
And to this day his love abounds

As years went by so swift
There was another added phase
Grandchildren added to the mix
With this our numbers raised

When this group grew up so fast
Begot yet another generation
The joy and love continues
Ensuring our DNA contribution

Thinking old age a bore
We soon learned not the case
With family, friends, and travel
We have a quite hectic pace

Thank you, God, for this all
The gifts of grace and peace
With lives of love and laughter
May this comfort never cease

OUR TROUBLED WORLD

Lord, guard this our vast land
From east to west and more
From north to south and also
To the far and distant shore

Where there is danger always
When the wars never cease
Heal this world of ours
So we may dream of peace

The troubled days of conflict
From every walk of life
Take greed and evil from it
Free the suffering from their strife

Until this comes to pass
Help us to do our part
Teaching love of brother
With a true and loving heart

Prayers to heal our nations
Is where our calling lies
Spreading God's true word
And from the depths of sin rise

A world with such plenty
Should provide enough for all
Erasing selfish greed
This is everyone's call

How to come about this
Only God knows the plan
Ask him to guide us all
To help heal this broken land

Our World

This world we live in
It is what it is today
Throughout history
Has been thought of this way

Wars and conflicts continue
As we journey on this earth
As man continues to struggle
For power and yearn for worth

Destruction and rebuilding
Each generation must endure
The task not of their making
But continues just as sure

Shattered lives and lands
Haven't brought all peace
We in our land of freedom
May dangers and evil cease

May all leaders of every land
Have wisdom to unite
To reach a common answer
That for all concerned is right

We must cherish our freedom
To worship, work, and live
The good life all lands deserve
Which wise leadership would give

Passengers

Passengers began so simple
Walking was the way
Jesus rode a donkey small
To Jerusalem that day

Donkeys, camels, chariots
Early passengers did go
Yet people walked most often
To travel to and fro

Horses played a major role
Carried man from place to place
To war and daily travel
Still hold riders as they race

From chariots to carriages
To ships that cross the sea
Trains came to the travel scene
Transporting all that be

Then airplanes carried people
Through skies to places far
The world became much smaller
In a short time there you are

Possums carry young
A pouch holding all the while
And kangaroos do as well
Passengers, nature's style

Trams carry passengers
High to a mountain peak
Submarines take you down
To ocean floors to seek

Daily passengers are moved
Wherever they choose to go
Man has devised carriers
To transport to and fro

Spaceships launched into orbit
Once impossible man did think
Now to the moon they travel
Now Mars, what's the next link

The passage that is surest
That we must surely board
Is the eternal express
That Christ's sacrifice assured

As passengers on this earthly ride
As we travel we must grow
With Christlike goals to strive for
We will reap only what we sow

PEACE

Peace that passes all understanding
This God-given peace extended
Our Lord did perfectly live it
This peace for our lives intended

This peace a source of order
This peace brings a calm healing
This peace so sweet and soothing
In this peace comes divine revealing

How saddened our Lord must be
When this peace is not shared
When broken lives fail to seek
For this peace his life not spared

From the simple peace in a home
A community living in peace
To other countries so distressed
Throughout the world should not cease

When power and greed come to be
Peace excluded turns to sin
Worldly gain giving no peace
An opportunity for souls to win

It seems that within all souls
The yearning for peace is alive
To acknowledge this desire
Allows peace the soul to revive

To quietly view nature
Allows the peace that it provides
Lovely rain, green grass, and sunsets
Among this surrounding peace we abide

So often forgotten when busy
Within our paths we don't see
Objects of peace God provides
Flowers, butterflies, and the bee

Take notice of your surroundings
You will be astounded every day
The beauty of people who share
Bits of peace if attention you pay

PERSPECTIVE

Not everyone thinks the same
Each person has a view
Take into consideration
Like thinking usually few

With this in mind then proceed
With your own personal thought
Then observe where one's path
Has not been as it ought

Such thought taken in account
Reveals, alters outlook
Perfectly clear to someone
Maybe a view you never took

The gift of this fair thinking
So valued in being wise
Teaching other ways conceived
You never did surmise

Take the teachings of Jesus Christ
Fair thinking too his strength
Take self a little less serious
And others' views at length

Two sides to every story
A hard rule to keeping mind
A precious gift when used
In addition wisdom find

Wise counsels use this guide
Keeping truth as the base
This always the bottom line
If indeed a fair case

The world has turned away from truth
The result a sad outlook
A change only when we turn to Christ
And remember the sacrifice it took

PLEASURES

Pleasures come in many ways
Since time began and still
Degrees of pleasure will exist
Individual choices if you will

Some folks' pleasures are simple
A sunset, rain, or falling snow
Some need more exciting events
To meet their status quo

Age levels make a difference
As to what pleasures may be
To very young are basic needs
While toddlers pleasure to look and see

As youths grow to teens
Their pleasures hard to curb
Temptations of want run wild
Some showered until absurd

Young adults' lifestyles
Are filled with growth and style
Cars and clothes and nightlife
Bring pleasures for a while

Then true love, marriage, family
Grant pleasures beyond dreams
A busy working time in life
The greatest pleasures, it seems

Seniors have transitions
Retirement, now just you
Travel or whatever
Free time you never knew

A farmer's pleasure is nature
Educators are pleased with learning
Law enforcements are keeping peace
While firemen prevent burning

Across the world a smile
Expresses someone's pleasure
As we all try to make this true
To all would be a treasure

POSSIBILITIES

Some things seem impossible
Out of one's comfort zone
Until the spark of realization
Reveal abilities never known

When young babies learn to walk
With small step approach begin
As their little legs support
Urgent attempts again and again

This concept we could learn from
Avoiding a personal unknown
To dare to venture outside our "box"
And claim it for our own

What joy can become ours
Discovering talents at any age
With just a little courage
To boldly conquer the next stage

As we approach each day alert
To things that interest one
It's the very time to begin
Things you wish you'd done

When each day is ended
It's over for all time
So make the best of it
A gift that's yours and mine

Preparing

Lights on the tree
Wreaths on the door
Lit Christmas tree
From ceiling to floor

Cookies to bake
Christmas greetings to send
Gifts bought and wrapped
But not yet opened

What's all the fuss
What makes us prepare
It's Jesus's birthday
We approach with care

Advent prepares us
With scripture and song
Announcing the coming
That's taken so long

Not to take lightly
We must tell the story
Our savior was born
And we give God the glory

The coming savior
Promised so long
Now came to save us
And right all the wrong

We rejoice with all
To celebrate the birth
That brings hope to us
And to all the earth

For young and for old
The message should be
Taught through our lives
For the whole world to see

So Christmas should be
The message so clear
The birth of Jesus
For us to hold clear

Preparation

To be prepared, a wise thing
In everything you do
Education, life skills, observing
Ask God to bless it too

From jobs to travel or projects
A plan in place, a need
Teachers, preachers, lawyers
For success in work indeed

Mothers, students, policemen
Preparation part of the job
Vocations all need attention
To a child, a class, a mob

Farmers, ranchers, bankers
Intense vocations of need
Affecting all walks of life
Financing and people to feed

All aspects of life need prep
And God prepares us all
With gifts we are to hone
Then follow and answer his call

Now God made the ultimate preparation
Along with his plan for the gift of grace
When he sent his son to save us
So one day see him face-to-face

PROGRESS

First the horseless carriage
Electricity and airplanes
Refrigeration for chilling
Penicillin for health gains

Trains for transportation
Hauling goods and man
The industrial revolution
Proving progress can

Telegraphs to wall phones
Television introduced the world
Computers, iPhones, and iPads
Into space rockets hurled

Music that was soothing
Turned into cater walling
Movies once so innocent
Now of death and mauling

The golden rule and honesty
Once the code lived by
Fails to be "politically correct"
Many no longer try

Family life quite often
Take a turn of fate
Trying to live the good life
See the damages too late

With all the gain and progress
Man has still a void to fill
Until we fit God in it
We will be yearning still

This verse not meaning negative
Of good that's come to be
It's true we have grace and peace
To be proclaimed by you and me

Rain

The rolling thunder
The lightning flash
The darkening sky
Rain starts to splash

One forgets
The lovely sound
The clean, fresh smell
Of the rains hard pound

It cools the air
It cleans the sky
Soaking the earth
Where dry roots lie

In a short time
The earth's alive
Swelled and moist
So all may thrive

Within hours green
So soon revives
Comes to life
Before our eyes

Be thankful for
God's answered prayer
When it was time
With loving care

This, too, will pass
Soon dry once more
Have faith he hears
Just as before

Not all feel blessed
Lives were lost
Keep these in prayer
In their great cost

Blessing for some
Though pain for a brother
Keep this in mind
And serve each other

Random Thoughts

When random thoughts come flowing free
Where your thoughts go, there your deeds
Take heed and sort just what is good
Cast from your mind and do take heed

Surroundings in your daily walk
Influence thinking to actions
Integrity and common sense
Prevent unintentional infractions

Living a life filled most with good
In touch with faith, what's true
Setting a pattern to emulate
The only right thing to do

Human struggle to succeed
In this life's journey told
Comes down to personal choices
As our daily lives unfold

Clean thinking so sets a pattern
If kept and direct our being
Taking wisdom from scripture
Reflecting what others in you are seeing

This an ideal way to think
And do the best we may
Being human we fail at times
To try again another day

Reality

The TV shows called reality
Leave something to be desired
Real reality can't be filmed
No matter how they aspire

We've gotten so far from reality
It seems we can't restore
The actual real and normal lives
Real reality was before

People in this world today
Lose touch with simple things
The need developed for much more
Is the thing that misery brings

To live within our real means
And not extend beyond
Our capacity to stay
Within our earning bounds

Seems like lifestyles change
As incomes grow too much
Values, morals, common sense
Can make us all lose touch

When people can stay grounded
And keep a wise approach
When success of any form
And different issues broach

In days to come, real living
Will be harder to maintain
When all the world is anxious
Extreme measures now to gain

There will always be a remnant
That keeps the faith and lives
In God's wise and generous ways
Content with what really is

Pray that we will be remnants
And practice simple proof
Only true contentment
Comes from this sacred truth

Reese, Child of God

This precious creation
God's angels sent
To join our family
In baptism we present

A child of God becomes
With water and the word
Everlasting in his kingdom
What joy looking toward

Surrounded with love
And shrouded with care
Protected by his word
This child so fair

Such a bundle of joy
May she always be
Laughter and smiles
For the world to see

With wisdom and knowledge
She will grow and flourish
Be a blessing to all
With a family to nourish

REESE

With pretty blond and curly hair
You have a flair your own
Such a joy to watch you
And the talents you have shown

Across the miles you show
Your greetings soft and sweet
Your time spent here so precious
To come to Texas is your treat

Remembering

A special day to remember
Those no longer living
Memorializing dear ones
Serving and life giving

Bravely answering the call
To serve to save our nation
A deep respect and reverence
Honoring each generation

Some gave their all
And remember all gave some
Among those who survived
Sacrifice escaped not one

The families of these brave
Along with them did give
So also honor these as well
With hardships they did live

The flag that serves our nation
Flutters above with pride
A tribute to those battles
And ones who live or died

Not just this one day honor
But each day give a thought
For all the past conflicts
For those did as they ought

As you hear our national song
It's OK to shed a tear
They join many shed before
For those we all hold dear

REMEMBRANCES

When we remember
The mind chose to retain
Memories that surface
Mixed with sweet joy and with pain

Here on our journey
Many things come about
Life's ups and downs
Filled with assurance and doubt

As we reminisce some of all
What is of the past
Happenings called life
And memories that last

Keep the joy and the wisdom
That come with each year
Glean from the outcome
Hang on to what's dear

Pass on the strengths
The laughter and truth
Teach from the mishaps
You experienced in youth

Pass on the comfort
That God was there
Keeping you safe always
No matter when or where

God gives us freedom
To seek our own road
Invite him along
He will surely lighten our load

Roadsides

With spring soon approaching
When roadsides come alive
With grass and blooms appearing
Among the trash will they survive

Now would be a good time
To clear the way of trash
Make our roadsides pleasant
If your paper you would stash

A container in each unit
Would be a simple plan
No cost to clear all areas
And littering we could ban

Speak of this to young and old
Develop respect and pride
Be the one to care about
Our God-given countryside

It will take an adjustment
For all, a level of care
Be bold and proud to lead
In this problem we all share

Roadside Trash

When will people notice
The trash strewn by the way
When will it matter
Enough to stop and say

It takes only seconds
To throw it by the way
It lingers many months
It's not just there today

The thinking or lack thereof
Shows a serious disregard
So simple it would be
And it's really not that hard

A filthy habit gone too far
Sends a message oh so sad
Generations could repeat
Not realizing it so bad

This sets a poor standard
For youngsters, adults as well
When it becomes unnoticed
We must the message tell

We all have responsibility
If each would tend their own
Reporting sighted trashing
Offenders be made known

If this is not corrected
Soon trash will be the norm
It reflects on one and all
A solution we must form

I plead with each and every one
Please take this serious plea
Keep a trash bag handy
It's up to you and me

Trash cans are stationed everywhere
Toss it in before you drive
Also eating on the go
The wrappings must stay inside

Satisfaction

Satisfaction is a broad word
Levels of satisfaction vary
The wants and needs of most
The choice that one will carry

A newborn babe is satisfied
With warmth and food and touch
As children grow they soon learn
That life may offer much

A challenge parents face each day
To teach of want and need
Limits must be determined
Thus preventing lives of greed

Individuals learn these values
Through wisdom that surround
Parenting, peers, and common sense
As tempting lures abound

The need for more advocated
In every phase of life
From cradle to world leaders
The cause for all our strife

The peace of satisfaction
With what our lot may be
And to remain content
A goal for all to see

Not to snuff ambition
Or growth, progress, or fame
Within bounds and limits
And not for unearned fame

When one has done their very best
And whatever goal they've met
Satisfaction is rewarding
And so have no regret

When viewing the big picture
With what is within our reach
Controlling our consumption
A lesson all should teach

The glamour, glitz, and promise
Of the joy that "stuff" will add
Will in the end reveal
Satisfaction we could have had

SAVING HISTORY

On the beautiful Yorktown creek side
Just off the then town square
The year of 1914
The town hall was built with care

With faith and hope in the future
Forefathers with true grit
Erected the impressive building
That's to this day deemed fit

Now the citizens of Yorktown
Owe loyalty to the past
Respecting the hope and efforts
Restoration now our task

With love and loyalty showing
Our historical pride and care
We humbly invite all citizens
Join our efforts now to share

The plan to create a venue
To serve town and countryside
Are soon to be revealed
And to all of you confide

We plead with all, consider
To monetarily assist
Continuing our worthwhile goal
Helping history exist

Searching

Searching delivery from the womb
Our first venture of discovery
From the first look around
And nine months gestation recovery

Our journey then begins
Searching in different ways
Some so serene and satisfied
Others search all their days

A gift this desire to discover
If none ever took this path
This world would ever be denied
The wonders the mind hath

The search for good a blessed way
To better this troubled world
And there are many works of this
As brotherhood unfurled

The search for better living
The search for peace and love
The search for generosity
As shown by God above

The search to end poverty
The search to end all war
The search to save the children
In this world near and far

Search to end greed and sin
To see the need of another
Search the scripture always
Love God yourself your brother

Search for all through prayer
God listens to every plea
He will guide all searching
He resides in you and me

Seasons

There are reasons for seasons
If you just follow nature
Since creation a pattern
That thrives as we nurture

The wind and the rain
The cold ice and the snow
All have a purpose
As nature does know

The sun warm and inviting
After winters severe
Some species not surviving
While others persevere

The object of nature
A cycle to repeat
Has its own timing
As not to deplete

As fauna and fowl
Root, bulb, and seed
All have a system
God's creation indeed

The soil rich and moist
The ideal we desire
Though not always so
So not always required

Natural ways of man and beast
Should preserve and extend
The future and beauty of nature
So to continue without end

Seconds, Minutes, Hours

Awake each morning knowing
This day, a gift these hours of time
I may squander it or use it
The choice is always mine

Each minute then accounted for
Used wisely and for good
Accomplishes something worthy
As well we know we should

This an ideal goal to set
Though humans that we are
Cannot always meet this task
This is what limiting time is for

Enjoy each task that comes to you
And think of it a good thing
No matter it's not your favorite
Such satisfaction this will bring

Separation

Time separated by day and night
Visually with light and dark
Earth separated by land and sea
All where God left his mark

Humanity separated by male and female
Creatures by land, sea, and sky
Seasons into four by plan
Sowing and harvesting is why

Newborn separated from the womb or egg
To enter life to thrive
Dead seeds separate from a plant
Into earth sprout alive

Separation of man and beast
One to rule the other
A balance God intended
Each species to serve another

The cycle of life teaches separation
When the teaching phase complete
Most living things practice this
After nurturing the cycle to repeat

Separations are a part of life
To understand and take is stride
Employment, education, and travel
Whatever situation you comply

Negative separations take place
When broken relations arise
A sad part of life lessons
When there is no compromise

The most glorious separation
Is when we leave this earthly life
To abide with God is heaven
Free of separation strife

Signs of the Season

A chill in the air
Leaves flutter down
Birds flying south
Grass turning brown

Football games
Fall festivals abound
Harvest gathered
Also pumpkins so round

Once a year this occurs
As sure as the sun
So welcome by all
Refreshing each one

The hunters prepare
For the annual game
Of who gets a trophy
Bringing them fame

Halloween, Thanksgiving
Again ushered in
Fun and sharing
Gather friends and kin

This cycle repeats
Since God created
His glorious seasons
To be celebrated

Matters not how many
These seasons we spend
On this great journey
His autumn beauty does lend

Not to take for granted
These seasons a plan
Nature at work
Guided by his hand

Snowflakes

As snowflakes flutter from the sky
Their fragile beauty showing
Soon joined by many others
Frozen with cold wind blowing

As they fill the winter air
Each delicate and unique
Gaining strength together
As through the sky they streak

So strong when joined together
Forming a frozen drift
A solid form resulting
Building strength quite swift

We as snowflakes are unique
Each with God-given skill
As we combine them for good
Many needs we may fulfill

SORROW

Words cannot describe sorrow
Although we know God cares more
Earthly loss is personal
When loved ones leave this shore

Human needs will surface
When one's pain seeks healing
Until intense hurt subsides
And God brings hope revealing

The loss a lifetime memory
Easing as time goes by
Living with it part of you
Recalling with a sigh

Memories cherished honorably
With comfort of salvation
With earthly death a heavenly birth
An eternity of elation

Each grieving journey so distinct
Needs respect and utmost care
At this fragile, broken time
To help one's burden bear

With love and sincere caring
One's own pace will then tell
Sensitivity and time and faith
Help regain spirit and peace as well

If the big picture could be viewed
At a vulnerable time as this
To know God's arms are open wide
To a sweet, welcoming bliss

When we are then reunited
God will time erase
From that time forever
Will live within his grace

Written to honor the loss of
Harper Shea and Kennedy Beth Carriger on August 24, 2013

SPRING

A spring morning
You feel in the air
A welcome time
Signs everywhere

There is this change
Surrounds us all
Coming alive
With nature's call

The soil gives forth
Its gifts each year
The growth it shares
To us so dear

The miracle of growth
Part of God's plan
Amazing to witness
Such a gift for man

A tiny plant
Appears from the earth
To reach for the sun
This miracle of birth

Buds on the trees
Turn to fruit or flowers
While others grow nuts
That fall from its bowers

The scent in the air
Is pure joy to inhale
This God-given sweetness
Each spring without fail

The grass and the trees
Paint a background of green
Added touches of color
Completes this scene

Spring '08 Madi

My prayer for you, sweet Madi
With each day I start
That you will realize your worth
A true love will win your heart

God has spared you strife and grief
That shows his plan for you
Includes a really special one
That you'll be devoted to

I know the age of twenty-one
Intense, extreme can be
Transition from the sheltered life
One day you'll clearly see

So trust the inner judgment
That you have always shown
You'll be ever oh so glad
When to that point you've grown

I have every trust in you
That you will be just fine
And then the "grown-up you" appears
That is this prayer of mine

Surrounded by Love

To look around you
And realize the love
That we take so for granted
Showered from above

The greatest love ever
God did send his son
To come live among us
Our salvation to be won

As we journey through Advent
Preparing for the holy child
God by his grace to save us
With his son a babe so mild

Too great to understand this love
God's concern and tender care
To teach us love for each other
And each other's burdens bear

To show this love beyond Christmas
Is the greatest gift we can give
Our gift to God to thank him
For eternity we will live

Allow your heart to grasp this
As you go about your day
Caring for each other
Spreading love in your own way

TAKE COMFORT IN...

Take comfort in the mornings
God kept you through the night
Take comfort in the sunrise
Created by his might

Take comfort in your family
Yours for you to cherish
A bond to walk the earth
Until that time we perish

Take comfort in a smile or a hug
It's the gift that keeps on giving
Doesn't cost you anything
And gives much joy to living

Take comfort in the sharing
Of time and talents too
This can so much accomplish
When one small thing you do

Take comfort in laughter
When heard it catches on
You've spread some needed joy
And sadness soon is gone

Take comfort in a good book
And share the knowledge sought
The joy of reading strengthened
Knowledge continues as it ought

Take comfort in your health
Protect it always with care
The comfort that it brings you
With nothing can compare

Take comfort in a handshake
An honest gesture shown
Given with sincerity
No better bond be known

Take comfort in God's grace
It's there for you to share
All you ever have to do
Is accept the gift so rare

TAKING A BREAK

Time away from the every day
Makes coming 'round so nice
When possible one should do
   This once a year or twice

Taking a break important
A change of pace is good
Needn't be a world tour
Stress free is what you should

A day trip to see some sights
Or an overnighter too
Whatever suits your style
Is just the thing to do

This land is filled with awesome sights
Places you've yearned to see
It's up to you to make a plan
To visit mountains or the sea

A quiet place may be your style
Or a place lively and exciting
So many choices from which to choose
What seems to you inviting

A cabin in the mountains
May be your choice of peace
A cruise ship to the islands
Or a high condo you may lease

Camping in a forest
With a campfire to enjoy
Getting back to nature
No daily pressure to annoy

With friends or family travel
The fellowship works magic
Relaxing days to unwind
To never take a break is tragic

TATUM

Tatum, with your pixie face
And eyes that light a room
With a smile to melt your heart
And chase away the gloom

The energy to go all day
Brings joy to all around
An angel as she lies asleep
Happy with love abound

Today you celebrate your birth
Two years have gone by so fast
Cake and punch and family
Legally the "terrible twos" at last

TATUM

Happy, happy, happy
A valentine for you
Just a little rhyme
In the mail to you

We love you and miss you
Look forward to a kiss
Someone has a birthday soon
And that we wouldn't miss

THANK YOU

Lord, thank you for yesterday
It went so fast
Again quite busy
So it didn't last

Good things happened
You granted that too
A hospital visit
And good things to do

You give me today
Help me to use it well
Stay with me and guide
Where I go and tell

Tomorrow as well
I'm sure you will place
Things in my path
To slow down my pace

Now slow is good
It's just not my style
Patient you've been
With me all the while

My prayer for today
And tomorrow too
Is to help me choose
What you would have me do

To choose you and yours
In my journey here
The best I can
In love sincere

Take my desires
And curb the excess
For you and for me
A simple life express

Thanksgiving

Colored leaves announcing
Thanksgiving Day is near
A time to reflect on gifts
So bountiful and dear

Giving thanks should be daily
Our hearts so full we share
Thoughts, greetings, all things
Freely showing that we care

So many thankful moments
As we rush about each day
When we stop to realize
Just what has come our way

Thankful God loves us all
And has and forever will
This alone brings such joy
When failing, loves us still

Family, friends, home as well
Sometimes we fail to see
Just how very precious
These gifts have come to be

When considering less fortunate
Whose basic needs not met
Opportunities for sharing
Such joy to give, not get

So use this Thanksgiving Day
To be truly thankful and give
Return the love God gives us
He will bless that way to live

That Lonely Walk

The Lenten journey ending
Prepared our hearts and souls
The lonely journey to the cross
Jesus's sacrifice foretold

The cruelty he suffered
The pain he gladly bore
To free us from all sin
Redemption to restore

God did suffer his pain as well
His love for us to show
The world forevermore to save
Assured salvation to know

The love God had for his son
He shared this love through death
We take this precious love we know
And share with every breath

Again this Easter morn we join
Our voices praise and sing
Our grateful hearts do worship
Our risen Lord and King

Until that time when we rejoice
Our thoughts follow his pain
Penitent and saddened humbly
Knowing his promise will remain

The End of the Road

At the end of the road
There is something there
However you travel
Consider from where

Your journey's launch
And a purpose too
Girded with provisions
What with that you do

Livelihood or adventure
This road has a reason
We go forth inspired
Each age as a season

No answers yet known
The mystery of life
Open to whatever
The outcomes are rife

There's no looking back
As we make our way
Wisdom with learning
Down the path that lies

This road is life
With which we are blessed
So many choices
Moving toward our quest

At the end of the road
If God was our choice
When the journey is ended
We will then all rejoice

The next road we travel
When we are with him
Will end the mystery
God was with us then

The Golden Years

Pills and treatments are prescribed
That "help" for all that ails
An entourage of doctors
Appear when one's health fails

The doctor asks if you wet a lot
You tell him you don't know
Compared with youth, you really do
Counting the times you go

He asks you if you have a pain
And relatively speaking
Yes, you have a lot of pain
And yes the bladder's leaking

Then the remark is always made
"For your age" that's not unusual
You bite your tongue and don't reply
Though the realization's brutal

And then go on to knees and hips
A toss-up that will last
Cherish them while functioning
As the golden years come fast

The back is usually first to fail
Because we abuse it so
Then it pains forevermore
Usually starts down low

Graying hair is next to come
Then call you sir or ma'am
You're one of them so suddenly
And proud to say, I am

Sight and hearing fade away
So slow you never know
Until one day they both fail
Who turned lights and volume low

Then the unheard, misread words
Begin to change the scene
When a statement goes astray
That's not really what you mean

Sleep becomes a problem
We just can't stay in bed
Three in the morning and you're awake
To the recliner you head

Arthritis had his way
He disables all we've got
Can't open, close, snap, or twist
When opened you forget for what

Obstacles are "planted"
We trip or sometimes fall
It's not that we aren't looking
"Don't pick up our feet," that's all

Technology is causing stress
The new ways don't compute
We learned the old-fashioned way
The young, this will refute

All are hurried here and there
The world just seems to fly
When we stop to catch our breath
The day has then gone by

Driving is an issue
It seems we are a "threat"
But we get where we're going
What's with all the fret

Inez and Edward had Kermit in the emergency room Tuesday evening and back to the doctor yesterday. He has sinus infection, dizziness, headache, and so on. And all tests checked out, so they gave medication, and he has to go back after Christmas or sooner if he isn't feeling better. We had good rain out at Cabeza and at Gruenau and are so thankful for that. Have a blessed Christmas and healthy new year!

The Greatest Gift

In this materialistic world today
Gift giving no longer anticipated
Overindulgence often why
True thankfulness is underrated

Simple gifts given from the heart
Needn't be of silver or gold
Thoughtful giving always with love
Gives a message sincerely told

So precious to ones remembered
When someone thinks no one cares
This is so very rewarding
The very joy when one shares

So think of the gift of our savior
God sent to bear our sin
Think of the love he shares
Forever again and again

This is the ultimate giving
One we should practice as well
Passing on the love shown us
Of God's gift of love we must tell

This the gift of the greatest joy
To receive humbly with open heart
Bringing the promise of assurance
Never then from this great gift depart

The Joy of Sharing

The gift of sharing
The joy it brings
Those never knowing
How the heart fairly sings

A hand reaching to give
And another to receive
A need fulfilling
With love will achieve

The giving be it small
No matter the size
The heart going with it
Outshines the prize

Feelings accompanying
The freedom to share
Without thought of gain
But to leave your gift there

When given freely
With no strings attached
A peace in your soul
A joy hard to match

Giving begets giving
It's a true fact
To be part of the cycle
Of an unselfish act

Any small giving
Will a great message send
Begin with tomorrow
Someone's need mend

THE LIGHT

The glow of a candle
The light from a lamp
The ray of the sun
A wood fire in camp

The headlights of a car
A flashlight beam
None can compare
To Christ's true gleam

Born to be light
To those who are lost
To case away darkness
At a very high cost

God gave his son
To pardon our ways
He came as a babe
And suffered end days

So when Christmas comes
To bring us the light
Let's take it with us
And keep it so bright

All need the light
To break from sin
And that is our calling
To let God's light in

It may be a word
A kindness so small
A helping hand
Available to all

Christmas bells ring
To tell of the birth
Of the Christlike light
Carols sing with mirth

God's gift to us
And our gift to all
Spreading the light
Such a divine call

The Only Forever

Forever, relative to some
Often misunderstood
In oblivion or denial
Achieving our own if we could

A subject much avoided
Our own earthly forever
We go on with our lives
In our chosen endeavor

Forever is just a lifetime
If this world is all we know
Only accepting God's precious grace
We may reap the good we sow

Accepting the only forever
Is a choice and way of living
Preparing our hearts and minds
For God's true forever giving

Salvation is forever
The greatest gift to achieve
We have an earthly lifetime
A free gift just to believe

Anticipating the joyous forever
Such a vision to bestow
To claim the glorious blessing
That anyone could ever know

The Power of Prayer

The power of prayer
Guarantees a return
Invest everything
What reward you will earn

A prayerful state
Is a good place to be
Calling on God
The results you will see

When we fail to pray
For all that we do
For others as well
Our faith to renew

There is praise to begin
And forgiveness we need
Thankfulness follows
And for help we plead

For poverty and loss
Illness and grief
Peace and promise
Prayers eloquent or brief

God always hears
Even when we fail
To call on him first
On our own to no avail

Accepting his will
Perhaps hard to say
Though he always knows best
And what we should pray

With him in our lives
We really can't lose
He's here with us now
And when eternity we choose

It's a win-win thing
If we walk in his way
Pray for the wisdom
To follow each day

The Power of Prayer

I greet the Lord each morning
And thank him for the night
Give him praise and honor
For the daily morning light

First asking for forgiveness
For failures in the past
Asking him to guide my day
And bless my every task

To bless this house and living
Family, friends, far and near
The ill, hurting, and lonely
And our lives you hold so dear

For leaders of this troubled world
For peace and lives preserved
That each of us may do our part
To help with needs deserved

With love and grace you shower us
At times we lose this sight
And still you remain right by our side
Though our cares often take flight

As we live just this day through
Help us do your will
To love our neighbor and ourselves
So we this world with love do fill

Keep all in mind who may not know
The love of God for all
Showing them that they may too
Count on him to call

The Reason

A Christmas carol
A soft candle glow
The scent of nutmeg
A red Christmas bow

There is baking to do
Presents to wrap
Cards to send
You can forget the nap

Shut-ins to visit
Shopping to do
Programs to attend
And caroling too

Friends to remember
Relatives to greet
Meals to plan
Adding a special treat

Shop once more
For that one last present
That is for now
And the crowds aren't pleasant

The tree to decorate
Wreaths to place
Lights to hang
What a rat race

Why do we rush so
We do this each year
To celebrate the birth
Of our savior so dear

Keeping the joy alive
As we go about planning
A beautiful celebration
Across the world is spanning

THE RAIN DID COME

The rains have come and quenched the thirst
Of earth and man and beast
The prayers of all have been addressed
All's well to say the least

The earth is swelled with moisture
The grass is sprouting green
The trees are sprouting early
Cattle fat no longer lean

Farmers set for planting
Around a limestone pad
Eagle Ford will not replace
Crops, thought they've been sad

The earth has stored the colors
To spend this spring with rain
To brighten all the roadsides
And every country lane

The greens are oh so bright
The flowers will be too
The grain and grazing rich
The rain will growth renew

This brighter spring is promised
And promises are made good
Lent to prepare for Easter
And repenting if we would

The joy of Easter looming
The wonder of the tomb
The pardon God has given
And erased the threat of doom

The Small-Step Approach

All that you do must be approached
Each thought and word and deed
A small-step approach a wise thing
Decisive steps reward to some degree

All that you do in daily life
Requires steps that lead you there
With wise and thoughtful thinking
Leads to successful actions if you dare

To rush in thoughtless blunder
Often leads to mistaken ends
Where with a little forethought
May avoid lost reasons and amends

If making this a practice
Your actions will show this
Though ideal not always able
As most endeavors not go amiss

This just random self-help
Not always able to carry out
Something good to strive for
And certainly think about

The Whole of One's Being

Something to think about
The whole of our being
Always taking for granted
Just what we are seeing

The miracle of creation
Nothing will ever compare
Science and attempts fail
All created with God's care

The wonder of sight
And the sounds we hear
Daily taking for granted
Precious gifts ever so dear

The human body fashioned
To function years on end
The bones and cells and all
With the capacity to mend

The very gift of thought
And a spirit sent to guide
And joy and sadness known
In this body does abide

The beatitudes created
Kindness, truth, and love
Just to name a few
All gifts from God above

The Wind

The wind of nature
A mystery still
It's never seen
But has its will

From a sweet, calm breeze
To a hurricane's gale
We are at the mercy
When in its path we trail

The energy captured
For sails to set
And crafts they move
And a course is met

Pollen is scattered
By the winds' will
Spreading seeds afar
To valley and hill

A soft, summer breeze
So cool to the skin
Making bearable hot days
If outdoors you've been

Sea breezes on the beach
To add to our pleasure
The sun soaking in
A true summer treasure

A cold, icy wind
On a ski slope high
Takes away your breath
To stay warm you try

The wind carries leaves
To adorn the land
Its colors cast
As a painting by hand

Man has learned to read
And track the winds' path
Allowing us refuge
From the anger and its wrath

Birds of the air as well
Navigate in tune to streams
Of the winds' path and voids
Simple migration it seems

So this wind we seldom notice
Is busy with its duty
Helping man and nature
Create havoc, aid, and beauty

When you see flags flying
Or trees sway in the breeze
Keep in mind it's always somewhere
To blow our hair, hats, and tease

It's laughing through the sky
Swooping down to see
Just what's going on
And where it wants to be

The Year 2013

Time to store away this year
A memory of the past
To recall another time
Thus forever last

Joy and tears of living
A time now past and gone
Taking with it precious thoughts
Others don't dwell on

Beginning now a fresh new year
With prayers for hope and good
Always positive in mind
As all new years we should

Learning from the years that passed
Would be a good, strong start
Strive to better life and limb
And matters of the heart

Resolutions come to mind
Be careful what you choose
Reasoning and common sense
Determine what you prove

Approach with caution always
Be optimistic and strong
Step into 2014
That's where we now belong

The Year of COVID-19

This year has been like none other in all our years of living! We have survived it all (for now), and our hearts go out to those of you who have been ill and lost loved ones. We have been blessed again this year despite COVID-19. Our children, grandchildren, and great-grandchildren have fared well despite church and Sunday school interruptions, lost jobs, virtual learning, distancing, masks, limited celebrations, and canceled projects and appointments. We have learned many valuable lessons. We were lucky to work in a trip to Hawaii in November 2019 with Sister Marlene and Robin as our travel guide. She really made the trip packed full of fun!

Kermit turned eighty-five this year and couldn't celebrate as we usually do but made him feel special without fanfare. I celebrated the fortieth anniversary of my thirty-ninth birthday. Kermit has trouble with his back and is doctoring with it since we are back home.

We were in Ruidoso from June to August again, and I continued therapy there (to recover from broken femur in December 2019 requiring surgery), and KC made it three months without going to the doctor.

Morgan and John, Kaylor (10), and McKinley (six) are still living here. John (mud engineer) was laid off but back to work. Morgan was working PRN worked through it all. Girls did homeschooling but are back in school. They have both been rodeoing throughout the pandemic and kept them active and outdoors safely.

Kendall, Jake, Reese (eight), and Lars (four) are still in San Diego and bought a bigger house; they are anxious to move. Loren and Natalie live in San Antonio as well and have bought their first home. He is a personal trainer, and she is with Medtronic and has been able to work from home the whole time. She is interested in cooking, and Loren has gotten into woodworking in his spare time. They came to Ruidoso to visit and loved the hiking and, despite social distancing, had a nice visit.

Darren and Tina are still here in Yorktown, and Tina is still retired and stays busy saving animals and helping her family as well as us (always on call). Darren is in consulting but was off for months but enjoyed ranching and taking care of our needs around here, fishing, hunting, and always helping someone.

Robin and Clay (retired) are ranching and entertaining grandchildren with chickens and pigmy goats, swimming, helping in the garden, cooking, and having baking lessons. Also trips to the coast to fish and some beach time. Robin loves the yard work, and with Clay home, they have beautiful landscaping to care for. They love the country and the ranching they now are involved in. Clay keeps supplied with fish, shrimp, and oysters.

Kendall and kids came to Ruidoso and then to Yorktown to spend a month safely out in the country with Robin and Clay. They enjoyed fishing at the farm and at the coast as well.

Reese had sewing classes, and Lars enjoyed everything the country offers. Jake joined them, and they drove back with a stop off in Ruidoso again.

Madi, Chuck, Tatum (six), and Charles IV (four) are in Hobson, Texas. They purchased a home there and teach in coach in Karnes City and Poth. They stayed busy teaching in school and virtual along with Tatum at home. C IV goes to day care and is a very busy boy and loves to explore, and they as well love to go to the farm with Clay and Robin. We are blessed with their visits as well.

Keary lives in San Antonio, drives for Lyft, works for Amazon, volunteers, plays sand volleyball, and is our designated driver to airports for out of town functions and to anywhere we need to be dropped off. She comes to Yorktown and is one of our tech-savvy helpers and is a helpful shopper too. She is taking a college course at this time to add to her A&M degree. She also loves Ruidoso and helps us with our locating there in June every summer.

I stay busy taking this all in. It is a joy to have four generations here and always something going on. We still follow school sports and functions for all families that we are able to. God has been good to us, and we are forever grateful for our blessings of family, among all other blessings.

Have a blessed new year!

>Doris and Kermit

The Yorktown High School graduating class of 1959 met for a reunion on Saturday, September 10, 2016. We gathered at 2:00 p.m. to visit and reminisce and pay tribute to those of our classmates who are deceased. Classmates unable to attend are Phillip Bock, Cleveland Stehle, Joyce (Jablonski) Parma, Rose Marie (Kolodziejczyk) Smalley, Betty (Harp) Ladner, Irene (Jendrezy) Galbraith, Joe Reynolds, Lawrence Stratmann, Edgar Stratmann, Edmund Ledwig, Betty Jo (Rohan) Haun, Lynette (Goehring) Davenport, and Donald Kramer.

Fourteen classmates attended along with guests. Classmates pictured from left to right are Doris (Schoenherr) Koehler, Taunyha (Patterson) Jacobs, Judith (Markentel) Vallow, Kraege Wolpman, Gloris (Kozelski) Seifert, Lorna (Koopman) Borgfeld, Lawrence Striedel, Marlene (Schmidt) Johnson, Loretta (Koopman) Burge, Georgie (Kurban) Jaeger, Alvin Warzecha, Mary (Machost) Hilbrich, and Joyce (Schuenemann) Ragnow.

Guests attending were Kermit Koehler, Wayne Jacobs, Judy Wolpman, Frankie Seifert, Henry Borgfeld, Jean Striedel, Gerald Johnson, and Rose Warzecha.

A catered meal was served along with cupcakes decorated with class of "59" for dessert. The class colors of turquoise and white were carried out throughout the room, with tables centered with large paper turquoise flowers. Memorabilia from days gone by were displayed and were enjoyed by all, including senior play, junior prophecy, senior will, a fifty-seven-plus-year-old cheerleader uniform and leather jacket, and yearbooks.

Classmates agreed to meet again in one year.

These crosses that are colored in various shades represent the multiple positions you have filled during your time with St. Michael's school. We are so thankful for your contributions toward the education and faith in Kaylor and her peers.

Things We Take for Granted

The things we take for granted
Like gravity, water, air
With not a thought given
If it suddenly were not there

Food so plentiful and good
We eat our fill (and more)
Shelter, warmth, and clothing
So much we have, we store

Family, friends, and fellowship
To call upon and share
Cars to drive, place to rest
Our needs are always there

A place to worship freely
And gather at our will
Free to openly speak our minds
For many years and still

We also take for granted
Abuse our gifts we show
Until one day they will deplete
Gifts some will never know

With stewardship rekindled
We could save this precious place
But we must quickly take a stand
To preserve the human race

God must be so saddened
To see the roadsides trashed at will
Polluted air, lakes, and streams
Forgetting the beauty we could have still

THIS PRESENT TIME

The past is past
The future will come
Just for today
Your race you run

The past can teach
The future holds hope
Just for today
With now things cope

This day here and now
Without worries past
Trusting future's time
Joy today will last

What will be will be
Just do what is right
Then the past and future
For you shines bright

Troubles will come
And troubles will go
Embrace them as yours
Handle as best as you know

Good times, too, will come
Cherish them and share
Those times so precious
Occasionally rare

So one day at a time
Come what may
Just for now
May God bless your day

TIME

Time waits for no one
It passes without fail
We may sit and ponder
Get it back to no avail

We may fail to keep in mind
Thinking time will wait for me
All the while it's passing by
To return is not to be

Take each precious moment
Cherish it and live
According to God's guidance
This moment only once he will give

Moments, days, and weeks
Pass unnoticed, spent
And one day we are jolted
Oh, that's not what I meant

I meant to live and laugh and love
But was busy and did not
Too late did I realize
That time was all I got

So with the time left for me
So precious, now I know
Forget the "busy" little things
And just let life flow

Awake each morning thankful
That he kept you through the night
To guide you through this day
To enjoy the sun's warm light

Then as you pass through this day
Be kind to all you meet
You never know just what it means
You've not walked in his feet

You see that life should be well spent
This journey could be cut short
"Well done, my good and faithful one"
Are words from God's own heart

To Be Content

Oh how to be content
To observe and remain in awe
Of all the planets, galaxies
Made, maintained by God

He gifted some to search
Beyond our earthly home
My prayer, with his blessing
These spaces now we roam

These findings such a mystery
In these other worlds he made
Does he challenge us to search
Would that his law obey

The heavens of our known earth
The limits in my time
But future man extending
Revealed by man's mind

A familiar place, this earth
We know and live and die
Where will future man reside
In God's divine plan lie

Only does he know and guide
If man seeks his will and plans
Time continues just as long
As God intends to keep these lands

Thoughts of this are not for us
We live and thrive with what we know
Future is for the future
We must preserve all good until we go

I must do what I can do
To live, be saved by him
With each day here and now
And God will reveal all then

To Family and Friends,

This being so late will thus be more factual. No need for rushing anymore. Just enjoy the last few days of holidays 2012!

We here in Yorktown are doing great. Kids, grandkids, and now two great-grandkids are all just fine. With four generations here, it is a joy to have some of them within the area to enjoy.

Kendall and Jake are in San Diego, California. And they are the source of our newest great-granddaughter, Reese Maray Sandage, born on December 12, 2012, around 8:30 p.m., weighing in at 8 lb. 2 oz. and is 21 in. Robin went out on the second, and Clay went the day the baby was born. They are doing well, and Robin and Clay returned for Christmas.

Keary is still in Austin in between jobs and looking forward to the next one that will be coming along soon.

Loren is at UTSA and doing well and will continue to do so. (Won't you, Loren?) Oh the joys of college life!

Madi and Chuck didn't get to be here for Christmas as their coaching responsibilities required them to be back the day after Christmas. We will enjoy them at a later date when we will be able to get together.

With Kaylor, Morgan and John live here and commute to work so we all have a hand in the care of her preschool, dancing, and Sunday school, but Morgan works only two days a week, so she is at the helm most of the time. Kaylor is crazy about her daddy and welcomes him with open arms when he returns from his days of work away.

Robin, Clay, Darren, and Tina are still living here. Tina retired, and this fall was her first not to teach or coach in twenty-nine years. Robin is still a stay-at-home wife and still enjoys her country life. The boys both consult, Clay in the area and Darren in north Texas near Oklahoma.

Kc and I are trucking along with more going than we intend to but just seems like there is so much in our lives, all good, that we don't want to miss anything.

We intend to go to Scotland in August if the Lord is willing and our knees as well. We will get to see the new baby when they come for Kaylor's birthday in February. We have been so blessed that we have nothing to complain about, but we do anyway.

Everything we have creaks from neck to ankles, but I guess that goes with the territory we have advanced to. I have enjoyed keeping in touch with relatives all over as well as friends. Bless one and all!

Kermit and Doris

TRUTH

Attempting absolute truth
A lifetime of intentions
From beginning in the garden
Began all these pretentions

Since the fall of man
The curse did us befall
Obedience still our mission
Responding to God's call

Since that time and now
We all fall short of truth
So easily the slip of tongue
A nature since our youth

If not addressed in childhood
Untruth can seem the norm
Once the pattern followed
A habit to easily form

Untruthfulness rescues us
When our comfort zone is tested
Without thought of falsehood
Continues if not contested

Thoughtfulness in speaking
Would avoid this easy fault
If all could accomplish this
Bringing lying to a halt

From speaking age to adulthood
What a wonder it would be
If only truth were spoken
And all written words we see

How trusting and simple
Life experiences for all time
Would be if based on truth
From your lips and mine

A sweet and comforting thought
A goal for which to reach
Almost a divine attempt
To practice what we preach

Sleep becomes a problem
We just can't stay in bed
Three in the morning and you're awake
To the recliner you head

Arthritis has his way
He disables all we've got
Can't open close snap or twist
When opened forget for what

Obstacles are "planted"
We trip and sometimes fall
It's not that we aren't looking
"don't pick up our feet", that's all

Technology is causing stress
The new ways don't compute
Having learned old fashioned ways
The young, this will refute

All are hurried, here and there
The world just seems to fly
When we stop to catch our breath
The day has then gone by

Driving is an issue
It seems we are a threat
But we get where we're going
What's with all the fret?

Union

Union, a general term
Reunion, from that word
Brings an appropriate focus
To gather, bonds incurred

Families when extended
Separated by miles
Students, friends as well
Reminisce with joy and smiles

Leaders of our nation
Reunite, decisions making
Which then affect the world
And the path we will be taking

Reuniting seems a positive
But a negative it may be
Depending on the position
From which you tend to see

But reuniting for normal folks
Is a happy reunion day
With food and fun and visiting
In an old-fashioned way

When we stray away from God
Reuniting is assured
He is there and hasn't moved
Because Jesus's death endured

As with God and everyone
Reuniting after strife
Is the only way for peace
In this our earthly life

VIEWPOINTS

Consider any subject
Then consider others' view
All points considered
Alike positions would be few

Debates, laws, and politics
Domestic civil too
Bring about differences
Not about what but who

Any conversation initiated
From here to national rank
Creates chosen opinions
We have diversity to thank

This can be constructive
If you listen with intent
To reach a common good
To this an ear be lent

Within a marriage also
This point be kept in mind
When any view affects all
Listening is best you'll find

A classroom or meeting
You will find this test
The wisdom to consider all
Your view and too the rest

Nature forms minds that think
And no two think the same
Take this to heart with everything
How viewpoint got its name

This could be second nature
If practiced in every way
A healthy way of thinking
On the right track all would stay

Walk with Me Each Day

If I would just remember
That you walk with me each day
I think that I would surely stop
And change most of my way

Though I'm human and not perfect
You remain my savior dear
Overlooking all my sinful ways
As well all the others here

Help me seek your presence
No matter undeserving I be
And when I fail to serve you
You are always there for me

The joy I receive from you
Is beyond any delight
Give me the skills to share it
And do well in your sight

For reasons that I not know
Straying from the path you lead
Is spite of suffering for this
When on temptations feed

Though I'm saved by you
On the cross the pain you bore
Please forgive my weakness
I'm so thankful to be sure

Help me try to understand
My role in this troubled land
And give me strength and boldness
Serve with your helping hand

Walking in Their Shoes

If ever giving honest thought
To opinions not our own
Stop to take fair account
Of what is to us not known

Taking in every walk of life
Different levels of ways and means
That derive from one's journey
Through their developed thinking leans

Right and wrong are general terms
One of which we select to live
"One fits all" is not the case
Respect for each should give

What is right for someone else
Not necessarily for you
A good thing to remember
Had you a foot in their shoe

Just a good reminder
As we go about our day
Take heed of where one has been
As each person makes his way

Often revealed when we learn
The reasoning not explained
Clearly shows our misgivings
Our shortcomings so exclaimed

Think how Jesus was perceived
By different ways of teaching
And God's plan all along to teach
His grace to all mankind reaching

WARRIORS

To honor wounded warriors
Should be a daily feat
Not just one weekend a year
But every day you meet

Think hard what they give
So we may live here free
Their lives and their families too
For America to be

We have a duty just as well
To do our part right here
Always give thought and prayer
Support and love made clear

Find a warrior to know
While serving far or near
Write and do some thoughtful thing
To bring good thoughts from here

Remember families of those
Who have had to leave all this
Support and help them in some way
For everything they miss

When you meet a uniformed
Stop and shake his hand
Thank him publicly, sincere
Till thanks spreads ore the land

Appreciate the sacrifice
When they come home again
Continue this for they still bear
Emotions, thoughts, and pain

WATER OF LIFE

Like a small lost seed
In the dry, parched land
No hope for growth
To grow tall and stand

Such are our dying souls
When constant we dwell in sin
Without the water of life
Not allowing our savior in

When forever all the while
Water life is ever so near
Within our very reach
Jesus Christ precious and dear

If when our own soul
Or another's crying plea
Find we are all searching
The water of life is already free

We must all make it our mission
Opportunity to make this known
To those along our path
As we all strive to journey home

Welcome, Baby Tatum

How happy are the two of us
Now this precious added member
Love created such a gift
A gift of life we shall all remember

To care and nurture always
Each stage of her life to greet
A family built on sharing
And obligations we will meet

For now a precious little babe
Entering this world so new
We observe her with loving hearts
As she watches from her view

We ask God's protection
For now and all her days
That we as well as family
With wisdom guide her ways

Surrounded with much family
Aunts, uncles, cousins, grands
With love and prayers and hugging
God's put her in good hands

WELCOME HOME

Days and hours and hours of prayer
For dreams to come true
Waiting for the precious words
We have a child for you

When our hearts were settled
And we came to greet an infant
Little did we know we'd grown
To a family of four in an instant

Double joy and double love
Given and received on sight
From the first moment on
We knew God's way was right

Again more prayers lifted
That this miracle will come true
At this point our hearts gave way
Only one thing left to do

Trusting God to do his will
And grant this precious dream
The time has to make it so
The right thing it does seem

Now all this love we have stored
To share with these precious two
Will make a life only dreamed of
For us final and true

These lives will be a testament
To trust God and his will
A witness to bring faith, trust
That dreams he will fulfill

Giving thanks seems inadequate
For this chance to love and laugh
For this we'll give thanks each day
For Leland and Sage Granstaff

What a Day May Bring

First a day brings dawning
Awaken to what may be
Eager for a good day
So arise, wait, and see

Whatever may await you
This day is yours one time
Joy and sorrow mingled
Some days all is just fine

How we choose to approach it
Can vary day to day
Some lives include variety
Accepting come what may

Some lives are very structured
Some muddle through somehow
What serves us best we choose
Procrastinating then or now

Each day should include good
Opportunities always abound
One need not look very long
Where these needs may be found

When a day does bring grief
Or strife that it surely will
Remember, this, too, shall pass
For now our best to fulfill

Most days bring happy busy times
If we start the day with prayer
And if this should not be so
Remember God will still be there

When this day has passed
Never again to be
Take from it the best part
Tomorrow again to see

WHAT IS LIFE

What is life
It is breath
With spirit
It is depth

An earthly journey
Since creation
To dwell here
This designation

Only creation
Could account
For the majesty
Who could doubt

The intricate life
Of man and beast
Earth and heavens
Nature unleashed

Beneath the sea
The life of a plant
The miracle of birth
Sheer strength of the ant

The depth of the mind
The beat of the heart
The senses of all
God's master of art

A plan he devised
And leads the way
To follow it
Till Judgment Day

What Is This

Something that is precious
Yet cost not one small dime
It's been around since creation
Will be until the end of time

It's good from birth till death
For young and old alike
A healthy habit practiced
For some a sheer delight

Will never be overrated
Available where one may be
Advised by wisest men
To take advantage is the key

In this busy life we fail
Sensible instincts must dictate
Restoring strength and spirit
Leaves the body feeling great

Take time for this great treat
It will always serve you well
Leave the busy life behind
Take a nap and rest a spell

What Would Jesus Do

Our commission is clear
Challenging us to serve
To share and to love
And needs to observe

To live in a state
Of awareness around
So many do exist
And easily found

Too busy we say
As we rush through the day
As we pass many chances
To serve in this way

Poverty and illness
People lonely and sad
We don't even see
With blind eye I might add

A pat on the shoulder
A smile or handshake
Is a good beginning
An effort may take

Greater giving may ensue
As the joy you give
Returns to you twofold
A good way to live

Do the right thing
In the best way you can
A precious thing happens

Spreading 'Cross the Land

Ask God's blessings
Then give him the glory
This love comes from him
As you live out his story

Where in the World

Where in the world is your world
Following your heart is where
Gathered within your life
Joys and sorrows living there

One's world created solely
By choices made each day
Observing natures playing out
As life journeys make their way

Most often subconsciously moved
By influences we're inclined to embrace
Forming worlds that suit us
With some choices hard to face

All and all this brings us
To worlds that we now own
Remain on the path we've chosen
Accumulated by all we've known

WHERE IS MY PLACE

The miracle of our birthplace
This world diverse and vast
The fact that we are born
In this nation free of caste

Regions remain to this day
With poverty a way of life
Never to know of plenty
Only of hunger and strife

In this world of abundance
To think that this can't be
Since the beginning of time
Of this we need be free

With open, grateful hearts and hands
This should be our task
To see that every mouth is fed
This in our prayers should ask

We so rich with many blessings
To see our children well
Never has hunger threatened
Or no way a thirst to quell

To share our full bounty
To lands across the sea
Also to our own needy
What we about should be

Asking God to show the way
To make this sharing true
Teaching a productive way to thrive
A quest for me, for you

Whom Do We Please

Whom do we please
Usually one's own
Unconsciously done
Why not known

Choosing works
A natural course
Mistakenly done
By our driving force

Our comfort zone
So easy to choose
Pleasing one's self
Unknowingly lose

When growing in grace
We soon realize
Pleasing through works
Will not win the prize

Grace teaches truth
That works alone
Fail God and man
For which we atone

Accepting God's grace
Through this true giving
Done with God's glory
Intended for living

The pleasing results
When we follow God's plan
The pleasure of doing
What God meant for man

WHO'S TO SAY

Who's to say
What's right or wrong
What's up or down
Or weak or strong

Who's to say
What's young or old
What's black or white
Or shy or bold

Who's to say
Who's smart or not
Who's short or tall
Or cold or hot

Who's to say
Who sings so sweet
Who's number one
Or skips a beat

Who's to say
Who's fast or slow
What time is right
High or below

Who's to say
It's night or day
It's rain or shine
Near or away

Who's to say
A relative term
Who and where
How to affirm

Who's to say
Christ is who
Our call affirms
What we must do

WONDERS

"Well, it's no wonder"
A phrase often stated
Negative or positive
It's often debated

"Wonders of the world"
At one time far-reaching
With modern technology
The chasm is breaching

"We wonder why"
And that's a good trait
We learn from our wonders
Which may determine our fate

"Will wonders never cease"
We hope they never will
Awe and wonder
Took us to computer from quill

"The wonders of nature"
Will always amaze
Who takes time to appreciate
At a sunset to gaze

"It's a wonder"
Gives credit to good
An observance takes place
We give respect as we should

"I wonder who"
Perhaps a curious note
But also opportunity
For a discovery or quote

Then there's "the wonder of God"
The greatest wonder of all
Nothing will ever compare
Or to us will befall

Praise God for the rain and all our blessings this week and always! I hope you can cope with the cold weather. Have a good week and all the season of Advent and Christmas!

WORDS

Words placed together
Create communication
Be they negative or positive
By who is enunciating

Sweet words of a song
Words make a poem rhyme
A letter longed for
A joy lost in time

An announcement to share
An invitation to meet
A thank-you so nice
Just a short note to greet

Words sharing joy
Or words bringing sorrow
Throughout life we read
Of the past and tomorrow

Words bring us history
Discoveries recorded
Created to convey
As they are forwarded

Words of kindness and love
Are the ones we must share
In this world of unrest
To show that we care

Now words of a text
Seems the world now favors
Losing face-to-face action
And the nice human flavor

Now the words to remember
Are from scripture and true
Read them, share them always
They're for me and for you

WORDS

First words are simple
A short burst of sound
A marvel to others
When a voice is found

The discovery of sounds
Associates with things
A joy to observe
The learning begins

Words form a language
Languages communicate
Interacting among people
Refining speech to articulate

Words and languages worldwide
All have a language their own
Different dialects as well
All identify their home

The gift of speech may take you far
Or one who's shy not so
The opportunities with words
Reveal knowledge you know

Words speak good, and words do harm
Wise use of speech will tell
Unwise use abuses speech
Past history's not gone well

Historically the use of words
Spoken once, forever live
Permanent results remain
A mindset that words give

Your History

History need not be of the world
Or country, state, or power
History can be your story
Beginning at your first hour

Milestones make up history
Your history to record
If only in your memory
Whatever you have stored

Journals are a precious way
To quote your journey here
To be shared in later times
For those who held you dear

Your need not possess fortune and fame
To make a history great
An honest narration told
Will a valuable telling make

Descendants who will follow you
Would cherish this endeavor
And honor your simple gift
To pass along forever

So births, deaths, and milestones
Should be stated to retain
Along with achievements and skills
Then in your history will remain

Talents, crafts, and callings
Of interest to those who care
To understand the origin
Of trends we later bear

So when we speak of history
Keep yours in mind to send
Into the next generations
To those whose lives will blend

This also makes accountable
Your lives as they will be told
Live with respect, honor, and truth
For our descendants to behold

Your Journey

Now it's time to take your leave
To go another way
Miles need not separate
As part of you will stay

Bonds were made among us
While your time here to serve
Leaves a lingering mark
Our thanks you so deserve

When the time now passes
And distance does us part
Think fondly of our time
As your new ministry you start

Our blessings now go with you
As your new journeys unfold
A little sad but for you, glad
Will fond memories always hold

CPSIA information can be obtained
at www.ICGtesting.com
Printed in the USA
BVHW051118180723
667424BV00006B/15